PRAISE FOR PARENTING
CHILDREN OF TRAUMA

Like Marcy, I was a trained therapist who had specific training in trauma-informed care, attachment disorders. I had worked with numerous kids of various ages who were adopted, or in the foster care system. I thought I was ready when my husband and I decided to bring our first foster child home. Instead, we went through many of the difficulties that Marcy described in this book. We were clueless, and my training failed me. While we struggled, I read resource after resource about parenting kids with attachment disorders. None of them rang as true as this book does! As I was reading her words, I kept shaking my head, and highlighting long passages. Marcy is RIGHT ON with her descriptions, her insight, and her applicable advice. I only wish I had this book when we had kids in our house!

I will be buying several copies and sending them to my friends who have children with attachment issues. I know it will be one of the best, most helpful books they have ever read. I have no doubt this book will validate their difficult experiences, while helping them find ways to love their children, and maintaining a greater level of sanity in the household.

Parenting kids with histories of trauma can be so very hard. Marcy's book is the best resource I have ever found to give parents concrete advice & solutions on how to make it easier.

—Mia

Don't do it without this book. WOW! What an excellent resource for anyone considering adoption, foster parenting or those smack dab in the middle of it. Learn from this expert. You don't want to go it alone and you don't have to. Can't wait to share this book with everyone I know fostering a child (children) or thinking about it. I may just buy 10 of them to have on hand.

—Marybeth

PRAISE FOR PARENTING CHILDREN OF TRAUMA

What an amazing book to provide resources for parents, foster parents and anyone parenting kids with trauma. This book is more than a lifesaver. It book gives the reader a better understanding of the different types of trauma and support for the parents in real, practical ways. I feel so lucky to have this book to share with my own community especially those who are considering fostering children. I'm sure that Marcy is saving many people's lives!

—Javier

I wish I had my hands on this book when I fostered 8 kids individually in the past! It would have made life so less stressful in diagnosing the child individually and educating my husband and I to fully understand and engage with them in the process whilst in our care. Very well written and detailed account of the various diagnoses. An excellent book to have for fostering in any home.

—Pam

Although this book is aimed at foster or adoptive parents, I read it in the hope that it would help me better understand a different kind of daughter – a daughter-in-law, one who had a very traumatic childhood. But as I started reading I saw things which I believe would be helpful for her AND for our other daughter-in-law to read for themselves. And then low-and-behold, I saw you describing things about me which I thought were just personality traits but which I now think were probably from the abusiveness of my father in my own childhood! So the bottom line is, I believe everyone could gain something from reading your book since who can really claim to be "normal"? Thank you very much for doing the research and putting your knowledge into a short and easy-to-read format.

—Linda

PARENTING CHILDREN OF TRAUMA

A Foster-Adoption Guide to Understanding Attachment Disorder

MARCY PUSEY

MIRAMARE
PONTE

Cover design by Happy Services

Author photograph by Jason Clegg

ISBN e-book: 978-1-948283-08-3

ISBN-13 print book: 978-1-948283-07-6

Library of Congress Control Number: 2019934649

YOUR FREE GIFT!
Get the Free Action Taker Guide!

Dive deeper with the free Reclaiming Hope Action Taker Guide!

This printable guide is packed with action steps that will help support your journey in overcoming the challenges of parenting foster and adopted children. **It also includes access to the private Facebook group: Reclaiming Hope: You are More than Your Trauma.**

At the end of each chapter, pull out your guide and fill in at least *one* step you will take to reclaim your hope.

Download your free Action Taker Guide at:

marcypusey.com/hope-action-guide

To every child I've had the gift of parenting:
I love you.
—M.P.

The Lord your God is in your midst, a mighty one who will save;
he will rejoice over you with gladness;
he will quiet you by his love;
he will rejoice over you with loud singing.

—Zephaniah 3:17 (ESV)

To the present foster or adoptive family—

Thank you. You are seen. Let's link arms and join our voices to bring hope and healing to families like ours.

To the prospective foster or adoptive family—

Thank you.

Thank you for picking up this book to understand trauma. Thank you for preparing yourself to be the best possible parent you can be for any child who graces your home.

Each one is a gift.

They need caring, committed, trauma-informed adults to say a brave "yes" to loving them through all of their pain and healing.

The contents of this book are primarily for parents who didn't have the information you hold in your hand when they began parenting children of trauma. So it's been rough. But what a head start you now have with this information!

In a world quick to cast away anything inconvenient or uncomfortable, you are considering your heart and home as a safe place for children who've experienced great loss.

Thank you.

Hang on to why this means so much to you, and to them, and let's change homes and families together, in whatever way you choose.

CONTENTS

INTRODUCTION

Many families are trying to raise children with complex emotional trauma, desperate for answers to heal and help their families. Caught off guard, these families find themselves with shattered dreams, shattered homes, and shattered hearts, with nowhere to turn for answers. Extended family members, friends, and the greater community don't understand the challenges and sometimes add to the problems the family faces, even prolonging healing for all. Failed expectations lead children to fall further down the spiral of despair, hopelessness, and trauma, giving their all to *survive* their safe and loving homes.

This book is for parents who feel embarrassed by their dashed hopes of adoption, confused about what went wrong and fearful about the future of their marriage, their children, and their lives as a whole. They feel overwhelmed, broken, and desperate. Sound familiar?

This book is for the wonderful-hearted people who stepped into adoption with dreams of loving a child to wholeness. Or for the friend or family member who has watched the unraveling reality of the adoption story of their loved one. This book demystifies attachment disorders, the impact of complex emotional trauma on our homes and society, and current treatment options. More than anything, this book will help the hurting adoptive family realize they are not alone in their desire to raise healthy kids and remain a healthy home. After reading this book, you will have reset expectations and new hope for moving forward.

I know this road firsthand. We began fostering children in 2007. Every single one of our foster children had distorted attachment. We didn't necessarily recognize it, but we fought to survive it. We adopted two of those children and raised them into adulthood. We have lived our own version of hope and hell in learning what real love looks like for these children. It took our marriage to the brink, our own personal mental health to its limits, our family to some dark places—but we came out in a brighter place. We surfaced with the support of our community, our dedication to *making it*, and a whole lot of prayer. It forced us to grow individually and as a family.

We have also lived in community with many friends walking the same road. Friends who knew their homes and love were big enough to be safe spaces for hurting kids, only to find that hurting kids *sometimes* hurt people. We've cried with friends and laughed with families. We've taken their kids as respite when they needed a break. And they've taken ours. We've lived our story, and we've lived up close with theirs.

Not only do I live this adventure firsthand, but I have worked in social services and therapeutic services for a *long* time. Before I was raising kiddos with attachment disorders, I was therapeutically supporting families who were. While it was totally different to show up for a shift and go home to my nice, safe house, I still learned a lot about what is effective and what isn't. I know the limitations which foster families must work within to bring actual help to their kids. I know the advocacy that works (and that doesn't) and some tips and tricks. I also know the disconnect between what we are taught as therapists and social workers, and the reality of the day-to-day living it. Trust me! *So* many of my school-gained strategies do not work with kids with complex emotional trauma. And now I know why.

In this book, I bring to you everything I've learned as a mama, friend, and counselor, with the most sincere hope that you will close this book feeling like you've been given a large glass of cold water after a long trudge through the desert. I hope this book feels like a hug and a whisper that says, "You are a good mom." Or "Dad, thank you for giving your best, it matters," even if everything around you seems to be screaming the opposite. You are not alone. Don't live in shame or guilt. Step out with me into a bright new day, with new eyes to see this noble thing you do.

Many other families, friends of family members, and social service workers have found this book transformational. Like this dad who said,

> I wish I'd had this book when we were beginning foster care. I always wondered if there was something wrong with me or my ability to love. I didn't know how much I'd have to reset my expectations and have accommodations in place to help me live in more peace with them. I wouldn't have expected them to love me in a way they couldn't. Or to make good decisions in life with so many emotional barriers. I wish I had my eyes more wide open going in.

Whether you're already in, thinking about stepping in, or know someone there, this book will help you: set realistic expectations, redefine love, and walk away with actual tools to change the climate of your heart and your home.

Have you ever doubted that you are a good parent? Through the journey of writing this book, and my first, *Reclaiming Hope: Overcoming the Challenges of Parenting Foster and Adopted Children,* I have realized that I am a good mom—and not because my kids are perfect, or because we have the most attached relationship, or because I figured everything out. I'm a good mom because I make mistakes (I'm relatable!) and ask for forgiveness. I show up again and again. I keep pouring. I say "No" when it's best for them or for me. And I say "Yes" when I can. My value is not defined by the behavior of my children. They don't prove to me whether or not I did the right thing in choosing to be their mama. This is a trap I fell into—looking for evidence from my kids that I'm a "good mom." Friend, if you're reading this book, you are a good mom. A great dad. A needed friend. Because you are showing up, looking for answers, for help, for support to help you keep your commitment to this kid.

You've given it all you've got. It hasn't worked? Well, you'll know why and what to do about it. This book will alleviate fears and doubts about who you are, who they are, and what your future holds. It will equip you with information, strategies, and stories to know you are not alone or powerless in your own home.

I'm so glad you're here. I'm so glad you're not like the dad above, who years and years in, realized how misaligned his expectations were, regretting he didn't have access to what you now have in your hands! What a gift that in whatever part of the journey you're on, you can begin to see your family in a new light with new help. It's never too late to heal our families, even if the only heart we have left to impact is our own. Join me in becoming a generation of families who hold our heads high and our kids' hearts higher as we learn what real love looks like. As we unravel the mystery of the traumatized brain and learn how to work with it and not against it.

Now, I know you've got a lot going on. In fact, you have probably had five interruptions just reading this introduction. Or maybe the house has gone too quiet. Or too loud. Maybe you're hiding in your closet or bathroom or car, grasping at straws in figuring out how to enter that space again with just a little more capacity to love your family well. I know your time and energy are limited. Believe me, I don't want to waste your time. Stick with me, a chapter at a time, and you'll be able to step back into your spaces with renewed energy, clearer vision, and answers to your hard questions.

I love you, dear reader. Thank you for what you're doing. Thank you for showing up. Now let's do this.

Section 1: We'll talk through the definitions and symptoms of the five major attachment disorders.

Section 2: We'll cover the impact of these attachment disorders on your family.

Section 3: We'll cover current treatment options and resources.

SECTION 1

A hero is one who knows how to hang on for one minute longer.

—Norwegian proverb

CHAPTER 1

ARE YOU GOOD ENOUGH?

I don't know about you, but when we decided to foster and adopt, we had high hopes. We didn't realize at the time, however, just how high those hopes were. In fact, they felt pretty reasonable. We fostered and adopted to provide a good and loving home to children in need. Beneath that reason was a belief that our "good and loving home" would somehow offer healing. Feeling armed by our experience with children, and my professional work with families in the system, we entered headlong into the adventurous world of foster care. There were challenges, for sure, but we were equipped! Informed! I was a Behavior Analyst. Throw me your behavior, and I had a plan and tools for changing it.

Against all of my training and knowledge, however, behavior tool after behavior tool fell flat on its face, leaving my foster children relatively unhealed—defying all of my education and understanding. Hair disheveled, hearts confused, we continued to pour and plan and pour some more because we were intelligent, loving people. *And we could do this.*

Except, we learned we couldn't. Our years in university and working in lower-income school districts with at-risk families did not prepare us to truly understand how to love our kids or truly help them.

That realization came devastatingly late.

After many years of pouring our blood, sweat, and tears into the lives of our kids, we were the worse for it. We feared that we were the horrible parents (and people) our kids alleged we were. Our marriage was on the brink. Our home felt toxic. And things were only getting worse. We sought help from traditional therapists and repeatedly heard that the issues were about personality differences or, even better, because we weren't doing enough. "Marcy, he's just not experiencing the love you have for him. I see how much you love him, but he doesn't feel it. Try buying him Peanut MnM's.[1] He says you only buy regular MnMs and I really think he'd feel your love if you bought the others."

I'm not kidding.

So we bought Peanut MnMs. And did the more listening, less responding. And the special-flavored snacks. And the lunches together every week. And every day the "thing" in the way of him feeling loved simply transferred to some other random thing.

We poured ourselves, like water, into cracked pots, our love seeping out of the cracks and crevasses. And all the while, the pot stayed angry and painfully sad because of how parched it felt.

I wish I'd had this book back then. To help me understand that we weren't crazy, that there were better ways of addressing these challenges, that we weren't alone, and that there were very real and valid reasons that our love not only seeped through the cracks, but also seemed to aggravate the problem.

The reality is, we didn't have this information ten years ago. Not really. For years, families have been told that *they* are the problem. That they just need to love more, pour more, care more, give more. And they'll know they are finally enough once their kids are healed.

The thing is, most of the kids we personally parented didn't heal in the timeframe we'd expected (or for some, at all). So according to many psychologists and medical professionals, we must not be enough. It's *our* fault our kids remain "broken," traumatized, lost. We failed.

What a weight!

Well, I'm here to tell you that this isn't true. You *are* enough. You *are* enough for what is needed of you at *this* moment. You *are* enough to love your child through one more day. You *are* enough to understand the need for help, to seek support, and to love in ways that matter. The outcome may not be what you expect or hope, but you still matter. Choosing to make this stranger's child yours when no one else was in line to take him or her is *enough*. Your love will not heal this child. Not because you aren't enough, but because of the trauma they've experienced and the impact of that on their brain. But your love still matters.

I know it doesn't always *feel* enough. *You* don't feel enough. You've given so much and your hopes are yet to be realized. You must be to blame, right?

Expecting your love to heal a child with attachment disorder is like expecting your love to bring sight to a child with blindness. There is more going on, and that's what I'm going to show you. I want to take the next couple of chapters to break down the dysfunctional attachment our kiddos bring to their relationship with us. I will walk you through the current conversations in the mental health community around attachment distortions so you are informed when addressing friends, family, and your community. I will also show why your enoughness isn't enough to heal them, and why it is still important. So drink deep and join me as we begin to understand what our kids are dealing with.

CHAPTER 2

UNDERSTANDING TRAUMA

One of the challenges of understanding our children's attachment is recognizing their symptoms for what they are: symptoms. They are not the core of who our child is, the sum of their value, or proof that he or she is a bad kid. These children are stuck in a cycle of trauma that has literally damaged their brains and it's not their fault.

I believe each human is created with the greatest value and worth. Our job is to learn how to honor that dignity in ourselves and in others. One way we can do this is to work toward understanding each other. To learn what we can of the other and make adjustments to our definitions of "love" and "help."

This is as challenging as it sounds! Even up through the last couple of years, people have argued that these disorders don't exist because they weren't clearly classified in the Diagnostic and Statistical Manual (DSM) used by those in psychiatry. It's always a work-in-progress as practitioners encounter new symptoms, new trends, and feedback from clients, their families, and society. However, the most recent revision does, in fact, include Reactive Attachment Disorder (two subtypes even) and other stress disorders.

Finally, some validation! But the conversation is still new, and we need every voice to be part of it. Even since the last edition of the DSM-5, the diagnoses are changing, but the symptoms and treatment are relatively the same. In the next chapter, I'm going to walk you through what appears to be the most current "language" around the topic and more than that, how to best support our families, our marriages, our own hearts, and our kids.

Let's begin with the top of the umbrella.

In the DSM-5, we have an umbrella called Specified Trauma and Stressor-Related Disorders. These disorders all share one thing: exposure to a *traumatic* or *stressful* event accompanied by significant problems in relationships at home, school, work, and society caused by the stress response. This means that a person's experience with a traumatic event is also getting in the way of healthy relationships, normal-for-them school outcomes, his or her ability to do a job well or to function within his or her family well.

In order to understand the distorted attachments that fall under Specified Trauma and Stressor-Related Disorders, we need to understand trauma.

Now, a traumatic event can occur in a number of ways. It can be a one-time event that threatened core needs for safety, like a natural disaster, an act of terrorism, or exposure to war. Or it can be ongoing *exposure* to a threat to core needs of security, like living with an abusive spouse, being drawn into sex-trafficking, or living with an abusive parent or family member.

Traumatic events don't always lead to trauma in the person. One individual may experience a traumatic event as a loss of trust and security, believing the whole world is evil and they can trust no one to keep them safe. Others can experience that same traumatic event and learn that some people are bad, and sometimes bad things happen, but there are still trustworthy people and good can be found on earth. The way an individual interprets the traumatic event will determine if the event becomes personal trauma.

It's worth saying that some traumatic events are so awful and violating that hardly anyone walks away un-traumatized. Some events are so strong in their intensity, duration, and frequency, that psychological harm is inevitable. So this is in no way intended to judge the traumatized individual for their experience with the event. The point simply is, people can respond differently to the same kind of event.

This is where it gets tricky with our kids.

Our response to traumatic events relies in part on the life experience, cognitive ability, and resources we've acquired to work through the event. But most children have neither the life experience nor the cognitive development to respond to trauma at all. Their brains interpreted their traumatic event(s) well before they had words to name it or resources to help them interpret it.

For some, their brains were interpreting the loss of security in the womb! At these developmental stages of the brain, an interpretation of "this person isn't keeping me safe, is bringing me harm, and can't be trusted" becomes a neurological pathway in the brain. The brain literally rewires to support this new belief that people who should be trusted can't be, and not only are they dangerous, but trusting them could actually lead to the child's death. So an attempt to be a loving caregiver can actually trigger the unprocessed trauma in the child's brain.

Let me say it more clearly:

If you have a child who falls under attachment trauma, your love demonstrated may trigger your child's trauma.

It's not your fault. It's not their fault. It's the way his or her early brain responded to legitimate harm in order to keep them alive.

Except that it's faulty and actually causing them harm.

This idea showed up in my home recently. One of my kids was having hip pain so we visited a chiropractor. After feeling around and asking questions, the doctor noted that a previous trauma to her ankle (she had sprained it a few years before) was causing pain in her hip. Why? Because when her ankle was injured, she compensated by leaning more on her other leg to protect the injured leg. This is exactly what she needed to do to allow her injury time to heal. It was *necessary* for healing. Important work.

But now that the ankle is healed, her body has adjusted to having a slight limp, even though there is no current injury. Instead, the limp causes harm to the rest of her spine, hips, knee, etc. Her body is stuck trying to protect against an injury of the past, thereby causing *new* injuries.

This is what it's like to be in the brains of our kids—rewired to legitimately meet a survival need. It protected them from real risk when they needed it. But now the risk is gone, the injury "healed," and their brains are still compensating to protect against an injury of the past, prolonging *true* healing.

This doesn't only affect the brains of adopted or foster children. There are instances of children born into loving and healthy families who have attachment disorders. WHAT?!

Yes. In one particular story, a friend shared her birthing experience. During labor, the baby went into distress. The cord was wrapped around her neck, tightening as the mother's body worked to deliver this sweet girl into her mother's waiting and loving arms. In this flash of distress, it appears that her daughter's brain learned, "My mom can't keep me safe! I'm alone in the world! No one can be trusted!" This daughter has lived her life in a devoted, loving home, rarely able to experience love or respond in kind.

Trauma, then, is when a person experiences two things: a threat to his or her life/survival and powerlessness (inability to change the situation). Fleeing and fighting are both strategies to overcome these threats. They each provide an opportunity for the person to take action to preserve their life.

When someone does not have a strategy, they are forced to freeze. Think of a deer caught in headlights. With no capacity to quickly decide between running or fighting, the deer remains planted to the ground, stuck. This is freezing. In the case of a mountain lion attack, freezing may save the deer's life. In the case of a car, freezing may *cost* the deer its life. If the trauma cannot be discharged or processed completely through the Freeze response, we have *stuck* trauma.

A threat to life includes an actual threat to one's physical body or life, but also includes the loss of a parent (one's connection to survival). Studies have shown that basic needs met from a caregiver are not enough.[1] As social beings, we also need connection and comfort. Without that emotional connection with a caregiver—even with basic needs being met—a child suffering from the loss of a parent experiences a threat to his or her life. This loss can be in the form of actual death or of access to a relationship with the parent through illness or dysfunction.

Powerlessness is when your brain enters the Freeze part of the Fight-Flight-Freeze cycle. When the brain responds with Freeze, the trauma enters the amygdala and gets stuck. Think Holocaust victims. As they watched their people suffer, fighting was a sure path to their own deaths, as was fleeing. Freezing was the only option for survival.

Importantly, the Fight or Flight responses both move the event into the hippocampus, a part of the brain which allows trauma to process in a more productive and categorical way. It also assigns the traumatic event to a space in history. The Freeze response is the only one to occur in the amygdala. This not only keeps the trauma stuck in a highly reactive part of the brain (hence the name *Reactive* Attachment Disorder), but keeps it always in the present.

You heard that right.

A person's trauma that involved the Freeze response does not get assigned a place in time and history like Fight and Flight. It remains present at all times. Have you ever felt like you're paying for the failure of previous caregivers?

You are. Our children's brains are leading them as though the trauma is current. Until it gets pushed through the amygdala, it will remain as true to them *now* as it was during the event.

Understanding that all of our adopted children carry with them a story of loss, a story of trauma (the loss of a parent, powerlessness to change their situation, etc.), can bring understanding and compassion to why their behaviors are so big, so appalling, and so contrary to their actual desires of health, safety, and survival. Their brains are working against them because of what they've endured.

The good news is that there's hope! With the right support, community, and connection, the human brain *can* process trauma. It can recognize that we did survive, that we are no longer powerless, and that our life was not harmed. It *can* complete and process the trauma. The traumatic event leaves the amygdala, goes into procedural memory, and then into the hippocampus where it can be chronologically ordered into time and space. It can become the past. This is resilience! Having the resources needed to move through a traumatic event to a place of physical, emotional, mental, and spiritual health.

Now, you might be thinking, "Wait. My kid has support, community, and connection, and his brain is not healing. In fact, every time we offer support, community, and connection, he goes berserk. This is bogus."

I don't blame you.

When we began fostering and then adopting, we went in with the full belief that our love and connection and good efforts would bring healing to our child. It didn't. At least not in ways we could see. All this brain talk sounded great, but we weren't seeing most of it play out the way we wanted. In fact, we poured and poured and poured, exhausted and depleted but still pouring, only to find their souls as dry and parched as ever. Where were we going wrong?

This is exactly what leads us into the next few chapters.

Let's now take a look at the five major attachment-impacted disorders: Reactive Attachment Disorder (RAD), Disinhibited Social Engagement Disorder (DSED), formerly a subtype of RAD, Post Traumatic Stress Disorder (PTSD), Acute Stress Disorder (ASD), and Adjustment Disorders that make up Specified Trauma and Stressor-Related Disorders. The following five chapters lay out the symptoms and definitions of the five main disorders.

CHAPTER 3

REACTIVE ATTACHMENT
DISORDER

A note before we start: It's common to find yourself or your child in every symptom! Especially when you yourself have been dealing with a level of trauma. The following overview is meant to give some language, context, and hope to families dealing with these behaviors, but in and of itself is not meant to be a diagnostic tool. If you suspect your child may be dealing with one or more of the following disorders, follow up with an attachment-specialized therapist or pediatrician. Find a support group of families raising children with these disorders. You can also utilize Section 3 on treatment for children and families dealing with these attachment disorders.

I have parented a number of children with this particular disorder, and I am either a friend or acquaintance to many others raising these kiddos as well. The wild thing about Reactive Attachment Disorder (RAD) is that many parents raising these kids have been told it's not real. They've also been very slooooow to receive an appropriate diagnosis for their child. I get it. If you don't live with it, it's hard to see or recognize. And if you're a traditional therapist who hasn't studied much on attachment, you're most likely being charmed and manipulated by the child. Our kids are good at image management and controlling their community. Therapists who haven't spent a lot of time treating RAD fall right into this trap.

Additionally, there are many therapists trying to understand just what this thing is. We all are. Some argue that the disorder is aimed only at the child's behavior and not what we, as their parents, bring to the relationship—thus being biased at its best and completely false at its worst.

Wherever you land as a clinician, the reality is the same—families like mine and others are struggling with some very common behaviors and we can't find or afford the help we or our kids need. While this argument keeps raging, we all keep suffering.

Historically, RAD has been the catch-all term for children dealing with dysfunctional or distorted attachment. RAD seems to be caused by a couple of different factors, affecting some children more than others. The reality is RAD has only been a formal diagnosis since 1980. The first time a cause was mentioned was in 1992. Research began around 2007. It's only been in the last few years that people are really taking the conversation beyond "Failure to Thrive" and seeking to understand why love isn't healing these kids. Traditionally, there have been two types of Rad: Inhibited and Disinhibited. The latter now has its own separate diagnosis, Disinhibited Social Engagement Disorder (DSED), discussed in the next chapter.

And recently, a new term has been coined in an attempt to capture the many nuances of a child of trauma: Developmental Trauma Disorder (DTD). While DTD has been denied as a diagnosis for the next edition of the DSM, you'll likely be seeing it more often. The comparison below will help you see the future of RAD as a diagnosis, and why DTD is a more helpful "label."

RAD is caused by childhood neglect or abuse, which leads to a child not forming a healthy emotional attachment with their caregiver. As a result, they struggle to form meaningful attachments leading to a variety of behavioral symptoms.

DTD is caused by childhood exposure to chronic trauma within the context of relationship. As a result, they may be dysregulated, have attachment issues, behavioral issues, cognitive problems, and poor self-esteem. In addition, they may have functional impairments in these areas: Educational, Familial, Peer, Legal, and Vocational.[1]

DTD eases the concerns of some therapists that trauma isn't significantly addressed in the RAD diagnosis. It also takes into account the many additional behaviors and factors resulting from the trauma, of which RAD is really only one.

As shown above, one of the causes of RAD, simplified, is neglect during childhood. The child lacked adequate caregiving. But this is bigger than whether they were fed or clothed and sheltered. This was the early mystery of Failure to Thrive. Kids had physical needs met but weren't growing physically, mentally, or emotionally. Research revealed the crucial need for bonding.[2] Did the child have a loving human who connected with them, convincing them that they could be kept safe from birth? This is *the big question.*

Much of the time, our kids come from birth families who either loved the child but couldn't care for them (and lost them to system involvement or gave them up) or were so caught up in their own unhealthy lifestyles that they literally could not love their own child. This is foreign to most healthy parents, but is a real thing. Typically, many of these parents have their own mental health challenges and perpetuate a pattern of trauma and attachment dysfunction when they birth children.

The other place this sometimes happens is surprisingly within some birth families. Yep, a few birth homes have children with RAD. I shared a story in the last chapter of my friend whose child was born with some distress and was eventually diagnosed with RAD. Healthy, loving parents can, at no fault of their own, raise a child with RAD.

In order for a child to qualify for a RAD diagnosis, a number of factors need to be involved according to the DSM-5. Under the Diagnostic Criteria Code 313.89, children with RAD must display the following for more than twelve months:

A. A consistent pattern of inhibited, emotionally withdrawn behavior toward adult caregivers, manifested by both of the following: The child rarely or minimally *seeks* comfort when distressed. The child rarely or minimally *responds* to comfort when distressed.

B. A persistent social and emotional disturbance characterized by at least two of the following: Minimal social and emotional responsiveness to others. Limited positive affect (think Eeyore). Episodes of unexplained irritability, sadness, or fearfulness that are evident even during nonthreatening interactions with adult caregivers.

C. The child has experienced a pattern of extremes of insufficient care as evidenced by at least one of the following: Social neglect or deprivation in the form of persistent lack of having basic emotional needs for comfort, stimulation, and affection met by caregiving adults. Repeated changes of primary caregivers that limit opportunities to form stable attachments (e.g., frequent changes in foster care.) Rearing in unusual settings that severely limit opportunities to form selective attachments (e.g. institutions with child-to-caregiver ratios.)

D. The care in Criterion C is presumed to be responsible for the disturbed behavior in Criterion A (e.g., the disturbances in Criterion A began following the lack of adequate care in Criterion C.)

E. The criteria are not met for autism spectrum disorder.

F. The disturbance is evident before age 5 years.

G. The child has a developmental age of at least 9 months.

Specify if: Persistent: The disorder has been present for more than 12 months.

Specify current severity: Reactive attachment disorder is specified as severe when a child exhibits all symptoms of the disorder, with each symptom manifesting at relatively high levels.[3]

As we talked about in the last chapter, the trauma process remains stuck, which these kids manifest through an array of challenging attachment anxiety behaviors. These behaviors are intended to be self-protective, from a time in their development that they can't even consciously remember, but which their brain recorded in their preverbal stage of development.

In a flash, their young, developing brains rewired to believe that 1) people in authority are the enemy, 2) that the people they should be able to trust will actually threaten their life, and 3) that they must be in control because they've had to be in control to survive. Expressions of love may create anxiety and anger, fear and resistance, to protect their very fragile sense of safety.

Robert Allan Hafetz, a therapist specializing in adoptive families who was himself adopted says,

> From the child's perspective, love means the act of abandonment will repeat itself. In cases of multiple placements in foster care, the response is reinforced and intensified.[4]

So what does this look like in real life?

It looks like your child not showing or receiving unprompted love and affection from you, but seeming to pour it on (or soak it up) from total strangers.

It looks like a kid whose world is flipped upside down, where every parenting strategy or instinct has an opposite response from a traditional home.

It looks like a child who is triggered every time someone demonstrates real love.

It looks like a child who can't even "afford" love because their trust is so wonky. (And the wonk is valid from their earlier experiences.)

A child who strives for their idea of safety at all costs, even if that means lying, stealing, sneaking, controlling, manipulating, triangulating, tantruming, throwing—whatever they think will keep them safe.

The main challenge for kids with Reactive Attachment Disorder is in their ability (or inability) to relate to others in a socially healthy and acceptable way. For example, children with RAD will either show indiscriminate affection (meaning excessive attempts at meeting needs for comfort and affection from *anyone*, even total strangers) and/or an intense resistance to initiating or even accepting affection and comfort from their parents (and sometimes other close friends or family), even if they are in distress.

As Hafetz so poignantly remarked,

> An adoptee will believe that he is in his forever family, but feel isolated and disconnected.[5]

Other behaviors you might see include:

- Detached
- Unresponsive or resistant to comforting
- Excessively inhibited (holding back emotions)
- Withdrawn or a mixture of approach and avoidance
- Minimal social and emotional responsiveness to others
- Targets mother figure
- Triangulation of loved ones: father against mother, community against parents, siblings against parents, etc.
- Abnormal eating patterns
- Failing to ask for support or assistance
- Destructive to self, others, and material things
- Failure to reach out when picked up
- Avoiding eye contact
- Steers clear of physical contact with caregivers
- Difficulty distinguishing who is trustworthy
- Difficulty calming down when upset
- Seems to have little to no emotion(s) when interacting with others
- May appear unhappy, irritable, sad, or scared while participating in normal (or even exciting) activities with their caregivers

If you find yourself nodding to the list above, it's very possible that you're one of the 10%[6] of the foster/adoptive world (I'm convinced it's higher) dealing with a child who has RAD. This realization is the start to getting your family and yourself the information you need to truly help your kiddo and yourself.

In the next chapter we will cover a former subtype of RAD, now its own disorder according to the DSM-5, Disinhibited Social Engagement Disorder.

CHAPTER 4

DISINHIBITED SOCIAL ENGAGEMENT DISORDER

I ronically, Disinhibited Social Engagement Disorder (DSED), formerly the disinhibited subtype of RAD, is the one I personally most commonly associate with RAD. Most of the children I worked with clinically who earned the RAD diagnosis, including children I've parented, and the children of friends, fell under this category of behavior. While I saw symptoms of Inhibited RAD in children I've parented, it was both less common and harder to recognize. RAD, as compared to DSED, is known for internalizing the attachment distortion, with fewer "big" behavioral symptoms.

In our experience, parenting a child with RAD felt like living in Crazy Land, where smoke and mirrors seemed to rule the day. It's normal to hear your child say, "No, that conversation never happened," when in fact it did. Or it didn't and you're crazy, just like they seem to think you are. This. ALL. THE. TIME. Children with DSED may tell you that events or conversations never happened (or did) but are less sophisticated in their tactics and are often so overwhelmed by their own behavior (as is everyone around them) that they'd be hard-pressed to convince anyone of their stories.

This is because Disinhibited Social Engagement Disorder (DSED) is similar to Reactive Attachment Disorder but is most recognizable by the *externalizing* behavior and a lack of inhibitions in behavior. That is, they display the signs more visibly to others and lack self control and/or self-restraint to do anything about it. They often lack the withdrawn behavior and depressive symptoms we've come to know in Reactive Attachment Disorder.

Like RAD, DSED occurs in young children when neglect and/or abuse have been present to the degree that the child was unable to form a close attachment with a primary caregiver.

One small study, *Disturbances in Attachment: Inhibited and Disinhibited Symptoms in Foster Children* found a higher level of physical abuse among children with DSED. It seems, as far as cause goes, that the expected attachment anxiety that comes with any child who has left the home of their birth, occurs in children with RAD. But kids with DSED seem to have even more severe traumatic experiences before, during, and perhaps after their removal from birth homes.

Let's take a look at the most recent DSM-5 diagnosis criteria for DSED in order to understand what clinicians are looking for when we bring our kids in.

In order for a child to qualify for a DSED diagnosis, a number of factors need to be involved according to the DSM-5. Under the Diagnostic Criteria Code 313.89, children with DSED must display the following for more than twelve months:

> A. A pattern of behavior in which a child actively approaches and interacts with unfamiliar adults and exhibits at least two of the following: Reduced or absent reticence in approaching and interacting with unfamiliar adults. Overly familiar verbal or physical behavior (that is not consistent with culturally sanctioned and with age-appropriate social boundaries). Diminished or absent checking back with an adult caregiver after venturing away, even in unfamiliar settings. Willingness to go off with an unfamiliar adult with minimal or no hesitation.

B. The behaviors in Criterion A are not limited to impulsivity (as in attention-deficit/hyperactivity disorder) but include socially disinhibited behavior.

C. The child has experienced a pattern of extremes of insufficient care as evidenced by at least one of the following: Social neglect or deprivation in the form of persistent lack of having basic emotional needs for comfort, stimulation, and affection met by caregiving adults. Repeated changes of primary caregivers that limit opportunities to form stable attachments (e.g., frequent changes in foster care). Rearing in unusual settings that severely limit opportunities to form selective attachments (e.g., institutions with high child-to-caregiver ratios).

D. The care in Criterion C is presumed to be responsible for the disturbed behavior in Criterion A (e.g., the disturbances in Criterion A began following the pathogenic care in Criterion C).

E. The child has a developmental age of at least 9 months (APA, 2013a). [2]:265-266[1]

So what does this mean? Simplified, this is the kid who will run up to a stranger, wrap their whole heart, mind, and soul around said stranger in the warmest hug and say, "I love you!" To which the stranger exclaims, "Oh my! You're the sweetest child ever! Mom, Dad, you are so lucky," walking off with their endorphins swooning and your child still crooning.

And then, you get home, and the child *you* know reappears, screaming at you, swearing at you, attacking you, accusing you, destroying his or her room or the house, attacking the cat, lying, sneaking, whatever "terror" looks like for you.

Now, is every friendly child likely to have DSED? Nope! Naturally, children learn to distinguish harm from safety and caregiver from stranger. Children have varying levels of friendliness and sociability. The difference between a typically-developing friendly child and a child with DSED is that the typical child knows that someone is committed to keeping them safe, and thus exploration is fun and a healthy way of learning. A child with DSED doesn't distinguish between the caregiver and the stranger, nor have a true belief that anyone else is responsible for keeping them safe. Ironically, their behavior can be perceived as an over-zealous effort to form attachments, by acting over-familiar with unfamiliar adults or new "friends," but not with the people they should bond with—their primary caregivers. And in fact, if any of the unfamiliar adults become familiar, say a school teacher, mentor, or close friend, the over-zealous effort to attach will vanish and the symptoms of DSED will present to these individuals as well.

Other behaviors you might see in a child with DSED include:

- Being highly selective
- Readily interacting with strangers, rather than showing natural anxiety
- Seeking unnatural comfort from strangers
- Exaggerating the need for help doing basic daily tasks
- Taking part in inappropriately childish behavior
- Appearing overly anxious
- Lying and stealing
- Cruelty to animals
- Destructive to self, others, and material things
- Over-sexualized behaviors in play
- Overly needy or clingy
- Difficulty distinguishing who is trustworthy
- Craving kindness from anyone
- Attention-seeking behaviors
- Sexual promiscuity
- Superficial relationships

If you find yourself nodding to the list above, it's very possible that you're one of the 20%[2] of foster/adoptive families dealing with a child who has DSED. This realization is the start to getting your family and yourself the information you need to truly help your kiddo and yourself.

If you found yourself nodding to both of the chapters on RAD and DSED, you're not crazy! Many children display a mixture of the two. They don't seem to be totally independent from one another, but have enough differences to warrant two separate disorders.

All of these behaviors (and more) will be discussed in further detail, including causes (to the best of our understanding) in Section 2. We will cover current treatment possibilities in Section 3.

In the next chapter, we will cover the third disorder of the Specified Trauma and Stressor-Related Disorders. This is a disorder that not only will many of our children deal with, but us as well! In my book, *Reclaiming Hope: Overcoming the Challenges of Parenting Foster and Adopted Children* I cover Secondary Traumatic Stress and direct trauma as experienced by the caregiver. We will go into more depth in the next chapter, both as it relates to your child and to you.

CHAPTER 5

POST TRAUMATIC STRESS DISORDER

Post Traumatic Stress Disorder, or PTSD, is much more a part of our modern day language. With so many natural disasters, acts of terrorism, and war, we may even know someone who is struggling through the symptoms of PTSD. We've learned that a singular traumatic episode, such as the survivors of 9/11 experienced, or a sexual assault, or the explosions that many Syrians are experiencing may result in changes to the brain that deal with memory, reasoning, and regulating emotion.

Because we often associate PTSD with a singularly traumatic event, many of us miss that our kids are dealing with it as well. Additionally, we are often suffering from the disorder, ourselves, and don't realize it.

For many children, there wasn't one cataclysmic, singular event we can point to that led them to deal with the fatigue, physical manifestations of stress, or anxiety that is so often associated with PTSD. And so it is for us, the caregivers, as well. What we can see, however, are ongoing and frequent circumstances that were stressful, even traumatic in their own right, that we or they experienced.

Certainly, being removed from their home is a big deal to children. But it's often everything leading to that removal, the every day "normals" of neglect and emotional abuse that created psychological confusion for our kids. I know someone who wasn't removed from his home and probably should have been. This person is an adult now and seems to deal with an even higher level of psychological confusion and emotional distress than children I've met who experienced the life-changing removal but were finally placed in a home with good, quality, loving care.

This is where Complex PTSD (C-PTSD) comes in. C-PTSD covers everyone dealing with symptoms of PTSD who have experienced extreme stress or violence over a long period of time. Going back to our conversation on trauma in the first couple of chapters, the experience of living with the threat of harm to one's life and hopelessness leads to the Freeze response, trapping the experience in the brain as "present." When the threat of harm is *continuously* present, however, feeling trapped, helpless, and powerless only serve to deepen the psychological harm and response, even after the experience has ended.

While C-PTSD doesn't yet hold its own diagnosis in the DSM-5, the conversation has begun, is totally valid, and is most appropriate in our context.

Let's begin with what the DSM-5 says about traditional PTSD, and then work through the differences of C-PTSD.

In order for a child seven or older to qualify for a PTSD diagnosis, a number of factors need to be involved according to the DSM-5. Under the Diagnostic Criteria Code 309.81, children must display :

Note: Slightly different criteria are used for PTSD in children aged 6 years old or younger.

A. Exposure to actual or threatened death, serious injury, or sexual violence in one (or more) of the following ways: Directly experiencing the traumatic event(s). Witnessing, in person, the events(s) as it occurred to others. Learning that the traumatic events(s) occurred to a close family member or close friend. In cases of actual or threatened by death of a family member or friend, the events(s) must have been violent or accidental. Experiencing repeated or extreme exposure to adversive details of the traumatic event(s) (e.g., first responders collecting human remains; police officers repeatedly exposed to details of child abuse). This does not apply to exposure through electronic media, television, movies, or pictures unless this exposure is work related.

B. Presence of one (or more) of the following intrusion symptoms associated with the traumatic event(s) occurred: Recurrent, involuntary, and intrusive distressing memories of the traumatic event(s). In children older than 6, there may be frightening dreams without recognizable content. Recurrent distressing dreams in which the content and/or effect of the dream are related to the traumatic event(s). Dissociative reactions (e.g., flashbacks) in which the individual feels or acts as if the trauma event(s) were recurring. (Such reactions may occur on a continuum, with the most extreme expression being a complete loss of awareness of present surroundings). In children, trauma-specific reenactment may occur in play. Intense or prolonged psychological distress at exposure to internal or external cues that symbolize or resemble an aspect of the traumatic event(s). Marked physiological reactions to internal or external cues that symbolize or resemble an aspect of the traumatic event(s).

C. Persistent avoidance of stimuli associated with the traumatic event(s), beginning after the traumatic event(s) occurred, as evidenced by one or both of the following. Avoidance of or efforts to avoid distressing memories, thoughts, or feelings about or closely associated with the traumatic event(s). Avoidance of or efforts to avoid external reminders (people, places, conversations, activities, objects, situations) that arouse distressing memories, thoughts, or feelings about or closely associated with the traumatic event(s).

D. Negative alterations in cognitions and mood associated with the traumatic events(s), beginning or worsening after the traumatic event(s), as evidenced by two (or more) of the following: Inability to remember an important aspect of the traumatic events(s) (typically due to dissociative amnesia and not to other factors such as head injury, alcohol, or drugs). Persistent and exaggerated negative beliefs or expectations about oneself, others, or the world (e.g., "I am bad," "no one can be trusted," "the world is completely dangerous," "my whole nervousness system is permanently ruined."). Persistent, distorted cognitions about the cause or consequences of the traumatic event(s) that lead the individual to blame himself/herself or others. Persistent negative emotional state (e.g., fear, horror, anger, guilt, or shame). Markedly diminished interest or participation in significant activities. Feelings of detachment or estrangement from others. Persistent inability to experience positive emotions (e.g., inability to experience happiness, satisfaction, or loving feelings).

E. Marked alterations in arousal and reactivity associated with the traumatic event(s), beginning or worsening after the traumatic event(s) occurred, as evidenced by two (or more) of the following. Irritable behavior and angry outbursts (with little or no provocation) typically expressed as verbal or physical aggression toward people or objects. Reckless or self-destructive behavior Hypervigilance Exaggerated startle response Problems with concentration Sleep disturbances

F. Criteria B, C, D and E last more than 1 month.

G. The disturbance causes clinically significant distress or impairment in social, occupational, or other important areas of functioning.

H. The disturbance is not attributable to the effects of a substance (e.g., medication, alcohol) or another medical condition.

Specify whether: With dissociative features Depersonalization Dereal-ization

Specify if: With delayed expression. This must be specified if the full criteria are not met until at least 6 months after the traumatic event; the criteria may be partially met during this time.[1]

Complex PTSD

Though not listed as its own diagnosis in the DSM-5, C-PTSD is being diagnosed by many mental health professionals and has been the catalyst behind a few changes to the traditional PTSD definition.

The reality is that C-PTSD has more long-term and extreme symptoms than straight PTSD. It's often diagnosed when a person has experienced trauma on an ongoing basis. People who are most likely to be diagnosed with C-PTSD are people who've experienced childhood neglect, ongoing domestic violence, human trafficking, kidnapping or prisoner of war victims, living in a region with war or civil unrest, or ongoing exposure to the trauma response/manifestation of others.

C-PTSD shares symptoms with PTSD, but also branches off into some symptoms of its own. People dealing with C-PTSD may deal with chronic fatigue, may tend to avoid others and have difficulty with relationships. They may find themselves thinking about death often (not necessarily suicidal, but intrusive, frequent thoughts of death), negative self-concept, and the more typical flashbacks, nightmares, and emotional triggers that manifest physically, such as nervousness, increased heart rate, nausea, etc. People with C-PTSD may find it difficult to keep attention, concentrate, or stay present. They may find they are responding to situations in an exaggerated way. They may also be dealing with self-blame, guilt, and confusion around the ongoing trauma, even to the point of believing they were somehow responsible for it.

I'm sure it's easy, in many ways, to understand why our kids might be dealing with C-PTSD. They had to—most of the time—endure a certain level of trauma to be removed from their birth homes. Even children who were removed at birth might exhibit signs of C-PTSD. While this may be rare, there's more and more evidence of the impact of in-utero experiences on the development of the child's brain and pre-verbal memory.

But what might be harder is to recognize ourselves, as parents, dealing with C-PTSD. I mean, we've had it pretty good, haven't we? Decent lives. Decent enough to believe we could bring a hurting child into our home and be a part of their healing. Relatively secure. A community of friends and family to support us. Life experiences and education to pass on to our children. Most of us haven't endured prolonged trauma for C-PTSD to make sense. And even if we had, and then healed, and are trying to help kids suffering from the same, we might find ourselves suddenly regressing a bit in our personal healing.

So let me help spell it out. When you took this child into your home, you had dreams. Hopes! If you are like me, you had experience with foster and adoptive communities. You spent time with them, either in your profession or with your friends or family members. You knew you had the means and stability to be a good home for a child. And you did!

When they first moved in, things were relatively great. You knew about the "honeymoon" phase, but really, they seemed to be doing well and so were you. When behaviors began showing up, you weren't too concerned. You could handle it. You had skills. Or at least access to resources with skills. And you knew that caring for kids is like a marathon, it's the long haul of love that pays off. So you kept pulling out your tips and tricks and pouring on the love the best you knew how. And maybe a little like a frog in boiling water, with time you began to feel cooked. Tired. Isolated. Disinterested in hanging out with other people. The front door opens and your palms sweat, your heart races. The phone rings and you hide. Your child grows up, moves out, and you have nightmares that they show up to visit. And maybe a little relief (or a lot) that they're gone. Then heartache that there's relief. Where did it all go wrong?

Friend, when you took a child with attachment challenges into your home, you took in a trauma. Your child manifests it every day in his or her own way, trying to survive. It's more than Secondary Traumatic Stress (STS); it's primary. They take all of their abandonment, neglect, fear, anxiety, and anger, and direct it at you in full force. Every day. All day.

Sounds like "extreme stress or violence over a long period of time" right? That's right. Re-read this chapter. Does it resonate? Are these feelings you've been having? Do you see any of this in yourself? It might be time to get some therapeutic support. And that's okay. You've fought a good fight. Your intent was noble and your love is not wasted. You've been through the wringer. Your kid needed you, someone who truly loved them, fought for them (okay, and sometimes with them), and showed them real love. They just couldn't show it, and that's not your fault. (Though, if you're like me, you're apt to replay your entire parenthood over and over and note all of your mistakes that might have led to this moment. Yeah, that's part of being a parent. And maybe some C-PTSD, too).

You've likely recognized some of these symptoms in your child. Honestly, it's to be expected given what they've survived. They've been so brave. So strong. They've lived through some crazy stuff. Hard stuff. Naturally, they'd be right up in many of these C-PTSD symptoms. I'll share some resources I found when I walked through C-PTSD. I imagine they'll be helpful for your child *and* you. We'll talk about treatment in Section 3. But before we move on to impact of specific behaviors, let's talk about the fourth diagnosis of the Specified Trauma and Stressor-Related Disorders: Acute Stress Disorder.

CHAPTER 6

ACUTE STRESS DISORDER

Acute Stress Disorder (ASD) may show up similarly to PTSD, but occurs within a month of the trauma and lasts for at least three days and up to one month. Its cause is essentially the same as PTSD: either experiencing or witnessing a traumatic event (or more), which creates fear, helplessness, and threat to life/harm.

A person who has already dealt with PTSD or ASD will be more likely to experience it again with a new trauma.

It wasn't until 1994 that ASD was included in the DSM-4 in order to provide a standard for mental health professionals to recognize and treat people experiencing early post-trauma who were at risk for developing PTSD. Research has shown rates of ASD in up to 59% for victims of sexual assault,[1] which represents a high percentage of the children we adopt as a community.

According to a study by Johns Hopkins University, the 530,000 foster children in care at any given time are four times more likely to experience sexual abuse than children not in foster care. The only noted exception is children in group homes, where the kids are 28 times more likely to experience sexual abuse.[2] I'd love to say that this is limited to their lives pre-foster care but unfortunately, children have been abused in foster homes, too. If your kid has been through multiple homes, as mine had (one had been in nine homes in three years), then the risk increases.

Clearly, our kids are likely to have experienced (or are experiencing) ASD in response to the traumatic events they've endured. Not only have many of our children experienced sexual abuse, but they've also experienced violent crimes, severe neglect, and the loss of one or more parent before foster care. One of the children I parented had "only" witnessed much of the abuse in her home, having been protected by older siblings from much of the chaos. Older siblings told me the ways they sacrificed their own safety to shelter the younger ones. Even so, this youngster I parented bore all the marks of trauma, witnessing things she couldn't even understand or have language to explain, all while watching her siblings suffer in her place. They've come from HARD places!

Let's look at the DSM-5 diagnosis of ASD and then spell it out in every day terms.

In order for a child to qualify for a ASD diagnosis, a number of factors need to be involved according to the DSM-5. Under the Diagnostic Criteria Code 308.3, children with ASD must display the following:

A. Exposure to actual or threatened death, serious injury, or sexual violation.

B. Presence of nine (or more) of the following symptoms from any of the five categories of intrusion, negative mood, dissociation, avoidance, and arousal, beginning or worsening after the traumatic event(s) occurred:

Intrusion Symptoms

1. Recurrent, involuntary, and intrusive distressing memories of the traumatic event(s).

2. Recurrent distressing dreams in which the content and/or affect of the dream are related to the event(s).

3. Dissociative reactions (e.g., flashbacks) in which the individual feels or acts as if the traumatic event(s) were recurring.

4. Intense or prolonged psychological distress or marked physiological reactions in response to internal or external cues that symbolize or resemble an aspect of the traumatic event. Diagnostic and statistical manual of mental disorders: DSM-5. Washington, D.C: American Psychiatric Association. Rationale for the ASD Diagnosis PTSD symptoms are frequently experienced in the days and weeks following a potentially traumatic event, but these symptoms usually remit naturally. The ASD diagnosis attempts to distinguish between these transient stress reactions and responses that may represent a precursor to PTSD. Early identification of individuals at risk for developing PTSD enables, in turn, early intervention aimed at preventing long-term dysfunction. Additionally, the ASD diagnosis facilitates access to mental health care (and insurance coverage) for individuals who traumatic event(s).

Negative Mood

5. Persistent inability to experience positive emotions.

Dissociative Symptoms

6. An altered sense of the reality of one's surroundings or oneself.

7. Inability to remember an important aspect of the traumatic event(s).

Avoidance Symptoms

8. Efforts to avoid distressing memories, thoughts, or feelings about or closely associated with the traumatic event(s).

9. Efforts to avoid external reminders that arouse distressing memories, thoughts, or feelings about or closely associated with the traumatic event(s).

Arousal Symptoms

10. Sleep disturbance.

11. Irritable behavior and angry outbursts (with little or no provocation), typically expressed as verbal or physical aggression toward people or objects.

12. Hypervigilance.

13. Problems with concentration.

14. Exaggerated startle response.

C. Duration of the disturbance (symptoms in Criterion B) is 3 days to 1 month after trauma exposure.

D. The disturbance causes clinically significant distress or impairment in social, occupational, or other important areas of functioning.

E. The disturbance is not attributable to the physiological effects of a substance (e.g., medication or alcohol) or another medical condition (e.g., mild traumatic brain injury) and is not better explained by brief psychotic disorder.[3]

The best sum of ASD is an attempt at catching and treating the symptoms of PTSD before it's full-fledged. While the ASD diagnosis has shown to predict individuals headed for PTSD in 50-75% of cases, it has unfortunately equally found that "fewer than 50% of individuals who meet PTSD diagnostic criteria [have] previously met criteria for ASD. Thus, the ASD diagnosis fails to identify half of the people who will go on to develop PTSD after a potentially traumatic event. Moreover, ASD's predictive power is worse in children than in adults."[4]

All the same, it's as good a predictor as any, and research is ongoing to strengthen how the mental health system (and friends and family) can catch the signs of PTSD and get help for their loved ones as early as possible.

If you have a child who has experienced a traumatic event within the last month, here are some symptoms to look for. Should you recognize them in your child, schedule an appointment with their mental health clinician and share your insights. A person experiencing ASD will demonstrate three or more of the following:

- intrusive memories that pop up at unlikely and unsuspecting moments
- negative mood
- Dissociation (everything from daydreaming, getting "lost" in a book, coming to and realizing they can't remember the last few minutes or miles, or as extreme as forgetting who they are altogether or taking on other personalities to avoid the pain of one)
- avoidance
- heightened anxiety
- decrease in emotional responsiveness
- difficulty experiencing pleasure in previously enjoyable activities
- feeling guilty about pursuing usual life tasks
- difficulty concentrating
- feeling detached from their body
- experiencing the world as unreal or dreamlike
- increasing difficulty recalling specific details of the traumatic event (dissociative amnesia)

In addition to the above list, at least one symptom from each category of PTSD is required for an ASD diagnosis. "First, the traumatic event is persistently re-experienced (e.g., recurrent recollections, images, thoughts, dreams, illusions, flashback episodes, a sense of reliving the event, or distress when exposed to reminders of the event). Second, reminders of the trauma (e.g., places, people, activities) are avoided. Finally, hyperarousal in response to stimuli reminiscent of the trauma is present (e.g., difficulty sleeping, irritability, poor concentration, hypervigilance, an exaggerated startle response, and motor restlessness)."[5]

If the symptoms persist for longer than one month, the person is diagnosed with PTSD. Early treatment can prevent ASD from becoming PTSD.

Now that we have a good sense of Post Traumatic Stress as a response to trauma, let's talk about the last cluster of disorders of the Specified

Trauma and Stressor Related Disorders: Adjustment disorders. These tend to contain the catch-all responses to stress and trauma that don't fit into RAD, DSED, PTSD, or ASD. Let's sum up the diagnoses in the next chapter before moving on to the impact of these disorders on our families and a conversation around treatment options.

CHAPTER 7

ADJUSTMENT DISORDERS

A djustment disorders, the last of the list, are disorders that are short-term (occurring within three months of the traumatic event and lasting no longer than six months beyond it). Everyone has a normal and healthy response to stress and traumatic events. A natural disaster or the loss of a loved one will always include a level of stress and grief. An adjustment disorder, however, carries a response that's a bit too much, too long.

In counseling, we have noticed that if a response to a circumstance is an over-reaction, then it's not really about that circumstance or issue. For example, one day I came down the stairs after dinner and a couple of our kids were cooking hot dogs. I came unglued. "Why are you cooking hot dogs right now?! We just ate dinner!" I went on and on about the hot dogs. I walked away from the encounter thinking, "What in the world? Why am I *so* mad about a hot dog?" After some careful introspection, I realized that I was on edge from a conversation I'd had that day with one of my children's teachers. Instead of addressing the conversation I'd had and working through the conflict that was presented with my child, I made it about a hot dog. We look for this kind of over-reaction in adjustment disorders as well.

. . .

Is your child's stress affecting their appetite? Their relationships? Are they avoiding people or important tasks that need to get done for their well-being? Has the major stressor ended and they're still feeling all of these things? It may be time to take them to a doctor, even just to get some feedback on whether they're processing the event in a normal and healthy way, or if they need some additional support. The symptoms of adjustment disorders usually improve with time and distance from the event. But if they don't, this is an indicator to get some support.

Adjustment disorders really cover six different subtypes, all of which share over-reaction that interferes with life as a common denominator. The six subtypes are:

- AD with a depressed mood
- AD with anxiety
- AD with anxiety and a depressed mood
- AD with mixed disturbance of conduct (meaning, the person may violate the rights of others or society)
- AD with mixed disturbance of emotions and conduct
- AD unspecified (You know, to cover everything else)

While each of these subtypes have slight distinctions, all adjustment disorders share a few things in common. For example, the individual will likely experience a mixture of four things: dissociative symptoms, re-experiencing the traumatic event, avoidance to stimulations that might cause them to remember the traumatic event, and anxiety or increased arousal/hypervigilance.

In order for a child to qualify for an adjustment disorders diagnosis, a number of factors need to be involved according to the DSM-5. Under the Diagnostic Criteria Code 309, children with adjustment disorders must display the following:

A. The development of emotional or behavioral symptoms in response to an identifiable stressor(s) occurring within 3 months of the onset of the stressor(s).

B. These symptoms or behaviors are clinically significant, as evidenced by one or both of the following: Marked distress that is out of proportion to the severity or intensity of the stressor, taking into account the external context and the cultural factors that might influence symptom severity and presentation. Significant impairment in social, occupational, or other important areas of functioning.

C. The stress-related disturbance does not meet the criteria for another mental disorder and is not merely an exacerbation of a preexisting mental disorder.

D. The symptoms do not represent normal bereavement.

E. Once the stressor or its consequences have terminated, the symptoms do not persist for more than an additional 6 months.

Specify whether: Acute, Persistent (Chronic)

Specify whether:

309.0 F43.21 With depressed mood: Low mood, tearfulness, or feelings of hopelessness are predominant.

309.24 F43.22 With anxiety: Nervousness, worry, jitteriness, or separation anxiety is predominant.

309.28 F43.23 With mixed anxiety and depressed mood: A combination of depression and anxiety is predominant.

309.3 F43.24 With disturbance of conduct: Disturbance of conduct is predominant.

309.4 F43.25 With mixed disturbance or emotions and conduct: Both emotional symptoms (e.g., depression and anxiety) and a disturbance of conduct are predominant.

309.9 F43.20 Unspecified For maladaptive reactions that are not classifiable as one of the specified subtypes of adjustment disorder.[1]

When an individual is experiencing dissociative symptoms, they are unconsciously separating normally related mental processes. The brain typically processes information in a holistic way, right? Where the various parts, though separate, work together to form one whole experience. When a person dissociates, these mental processes are working independently from one another and not communicating with each other. This potentially leads to an individual experiencing one of the following:

- feeling detached or emotionally numb,
- finding themselves in a moment where they have no memory of the last chunk of time,
- finding themselves in a familiar environment which suddenly feels strange or unreal to them,
- hearing their thoughts or emotions as foreign or even as someone else's thoughts, or even forms of amnesia where important aspects of the traumatic event is forgotten.

These are just a handful of dissociative symptoms that someone working through an adjustment disorder might experience.

This individual will also persistently re-experience their traumatic event in one or more of the following ways. They might re-experience their trauma through a flashback, as we often see in films with war vets. This might be through a sound or smell or time of year that suddenly sends the person back to the moment of their traumatic event. They might feel as though they are actually reliving the event, as real as when it happened, losing touch with the here and now. They might have nightmares, daymares, intruding thoughts, or other recurring images that cause them to revisit the moment of their trauma.

Additionally, individuals with adjustment disorders often avoid triggers or stimuli that remind them or cause them to re-experience the traumatic event. They might avoid people, certain conversation topics (or conversation altogether), experiencing certain feelings, thoughts, certain objects or places. They might avoid activities, even ones they once enjoyed, or certain smells and sounds. This of course is their way of avoiding pain, the pain of re-living the deeply scarring events that were perceived threats to their own lives or the lives of loved ones.

This can also show up as a time of day or a time of year. Have you ever noticed that your kid melts during birthday parties? Or Christmas? Or on rainy days? Or mealtimes? For many of our kids, their brains associate the trauma they experienced with a particular event, or a season of the year, or certain smells or foods. Start to jot down your child's disruptions and pay attention to any patterns that show up.

Finally, a person dealing with an adjustment disorder will often struggle with an increase in anxiety and arousal. This person may struggle to fall asleep or stay asleep. They might be irritable (I know I am if my sleep is disrupted!), have trouble concentrating or focusing, or feel on edge all the time. They might feel restless, on guard, and thus, easily startled. Their brain and body are on hyper-alert, ready to protect themselves at the first sign of danger. This level of hypervigilance is exhausting, debilitating, and prevents peace and rest.

By now, whether it's RAD, DSED, PTSD, ASD, or an adjustment disorder, you're probably noticing a theme among the symptoms. You might even recognize symptoms here that you are familiar with in other disorders. For example, many of these disorders are diagnosed in children as Borderline Personality Disorder or Narcissistic Personality Disorder. Sometimes a child is labeled depressed and thus medicated. Or sometimes they're just called deviant and caregivers try to punish the behaviors out of the child.

An additional challenge is that very rarely does the child have only one of these disorders. Very often, a child working through traumatic events is dealing with PTSD or ASD, RAD or DSED, ADHD, oppositional defiance, fetal alcohol syndrome, sensory processing disorders, or any other number of challenges. It can be very trying to figure out what exactly is leading our kids to behave the way they do and how to get them the help they need.

Thus, learning about these common responses to trauma is really just the beginning. Learning that trauma has a huge impact on the neurological abilities of our kids, their behavior at home and in society, and the toll that takes on a family is an absolute *must*.

Thank you for being willing to study your kids, excelling in the uniqueness of who they are, in all the wonderful and painful combined. This is the start of a new beginning! So let's keep going! The next two chapters dive into the importance of a healthy brain and ways our kids manifest their survival skills. From there we will look at the impact of a brain stuck in trauma and some possibilities around healing and hope for your family.

CHAPTER 8

THE POWER OF THE PREFRONTAL CORTEX

Wow, we've walked through some pretty heavy diagnoses. These challenges are not for the faint of heart, but you already knew that. When you signed up to foster or adopt, you knew these kids came from hard places. If you were like us, you were ready to love them to health and healing. I saw a lot of growth in families I worked with over the years, so surely I could do it with my own placements. And then the honeymoon ended and the behaviors hit us like a tsunami. But that was okay, we were equipped for this, right?

As Christ-followers, we especially had a sense that His strength and unconditional love would overcome every hurdle. I won't say it didn't, but I will say the challenges were far greater than we were actually equipped for. All of our knowledge and experience may have given us a leg up, but it sure didn't prevent the crazy and chaos we struggled through for many years. A friend recently pointed out a story of Jesus that I found profound. Jesus was praying in the Garden of Gethsemane, asking that God would provide a way out of the intense beatings and murder he would soon experience. And then Luke 22:43-44 (NIV) says, "An angel from heaven appeared to him and strengthened him.

And being in anguish, he prayed more earnestly, and his sweat was like drops of blood falling to the ground."

Jesus, in a most desperate hour, was strengthened by an angel, and having been strengthened, continued on in anguish to the point of Hematohidrosis, or bleeding from sweat glands.

If you share our faith and have believed that God's love and strength would make this easy, take heart. *God's strength does not mean the path will be easy.* But it does mean you're not alone.

While God's unconditional strength is *why* endured as much as we have, we still haven't seen the healing we had expected and hoped for in our kids. Not yet. But more on that in chapter 17.

We need to be strengthened if we are going to love our kids through their distorted attachment. While the journey won't be easy, our kids need us to keep showing up.

The brain of a child of trauma often has a very dark prefrontal cortex (PFC). This is the part of your brain right behind your forehead. It's also known as the "thinking center." It's responsible for really important things like being able to think rationally or logically, problem-solving, goal-planning, impulse control, being able to delay gratification, empathy, and self-awareness. It's the part of the brain that when lit up, enables us to make good decisions, have healthy relationships, live from the strengths of our personality, set and achieve goals, and think clearly. Few to none of these functions happen with our trauma kids because that all-important portion of the brain is dark—unable to do its job.

What does that look like in day-to-day living?

One child I parented could not say "No" to himself, ever. No matter how painful the natural consequence was or how disappointed his teachers, friends, or we might be, if an opportunity came that tickled his fancy in any way, he was all over it, no matter the cost.

Another child I know, around five years old, continually opens the front door and leaves the house. Her parents took time to train her to not touch the doorknob (let alone unlock it, turn it, and leave the house). They stood by the door and every time she touched it, she was disciplined, and they said, "No sweetie, do not touch the doorknob." She looked at them, maybe a tear in her eye, took a deep breath... and did it again. And again. And again. Hundreds of times. Even though she knew that discipline and disapproval were coming, she couldn't *not* touch the door. Her PFC was turned off.

That's perhaps a silly example, but multiply that over every decision that a child is forced to make every day, forever. And when you are parenting that child—AH! You can't turn your back. Raising a child with a dark PFC is exhausting.

There are a couple of reasons a prefrontal cortex will be dark. First, in some of these children, the trauma was so severe that the prefrontal cortex just didn't develop. It's not there. In these cases, the brain needs help developing networks to make up for the missing functions.

The second reason some of these children have a dark PFC is that it's unengaged. It's there. It's physically developed. But because of the trauma, the ways the brain created new neurological pathways to survive the horrors they experienced, it's completely bypassed. And all that bypassing over the years has numbed it out, turned it off. The good news is that studies are showing that dark parts of the brain can be re-engaged! It's a long process, but it's possible. We saw it in small (but meaningful) ways with one of the kids we parented.

One foster child (eight years old) was raised alongside a healthy biological child (toddler). As the toddler hit cognitive and developmental milestones, the eight-year-old hit them a few days later. Something about doing life alongside a neurotypical child encouraged the traumatized brain to pick up and fill in some gaps. This didn't bring full healing to the foster kiddo, but we definitely saw some new milestones occur for him, like being able to follow instructions with two or more steps or showing concern for a friend.

Having a fully functioning prefrontal cortex leads to making good choices, the ability to say "No" to oneself, and setting and achieving goals. It's also the center for morality. So not having the PFC functioning leads to many of the behaviors our kids experience. If we understand that our kids essentially have a brain that needs to heal from actual damage, to re-pave new pathways, and to grow—even though their overall behavior significantly impacts the whole family— perhaps we'll be able to remember that it's not us against the child, but instead it's us and them against the result of trauma they've experienced. While not every brain responds in this way, many kids' brains do, so here we are.

In addition to lacking PFC activity, we have to remember that our kids are often functioning from their amygdala, where the trauma is stuck in a "now" category. So not only do they have very little (if any) capacity to perform PFC activities when they *aren't* triggered, but when they are living from "I'm going to be harmed" all the time, they can only respond with their personal survival skills. Some of these skills might have actually kept them alive in previous homes, but now no longer serve a real purpose. Not only do these skills no longer serve them, they often cause harm in new experiences: not being able to form healthy relationships or connections to build the community they need to process through the trauma. When a child gets passed from home to home, the false belief that no one can be trusted is reinforced in the brain. This certainly gets in the way of any healthy attachment!

So when you come along and demonstrate love to that child, you inadvertently trigger their amygdala to flood with warning sirens, telling their body that they are in danger. Cue survival skills. Cue every behavior that challenges us, their parents and friends and teachers, to our cores.

Now that we have a bit of an understanding of the major, underlying cause of certain trauma behaviors, and the ways it prevents attachment, let's take a look at how those behaviors manifest and ways we can understand and address them.

CHAPTER 9

SURVIVAL SKILLS

I've taken the many manifestations of a trauma kid's survival skills and summed them up into four main categories: their response to logic or reason, their high sense of power, their "present-only" focus, and their disconnected thinking. These are not exhaustive, but are helpful in understanding what motivates their behavior and why that continues to prevent healthy attachment in their lives.

RESPONSE TO LOGIC OR REASON

Children of trauma don't have the executive functions of the prefrontal cortex to support reasoning, especially when their amygdala is being hijacked and flooded with adrenaline. This means that gaining information won't change your child or improve their behavior. This is true for most people, but especially for these kiddos. We also know that the most effective brain healing that occurs, does so with experience and not straight information. The child must experience, again and again (and again and again), true safety in order to begin healing. (This sounds easy, but believe me, it's not!)

This often shows up in arguments over petty things. Here is an example: A child of yours makes a poor choice involving candy bars from a fundraiser. You address the situation by asking, "Why did you take your brother's candy bars? What happened to *your* candy bars for the school fundraiser?" And you might get a very disconnected, strange re-telling of events with lots of holes and inconsistencies. So you'll ask a clarifying question to understand a gap in the story. Or, you'll immediately recognize the gap and try to help guide your child to understanding their faulty reasoning. "So you ate *your* candy bars and needed to replace them. Therefore, you told your brother the bars had been stolen. He then gave you *his* candy bars, leaving him with 3 of the 20. And you... kept eating the replacements?" You, as the parent, may or may not get a "Yes" to that question. Which you may or may not follow up with, "Where are you planning to get the money to replace those candy bars? You know, the money you'll have to turn in at the end of the fundraiser?" You will not be able to guide a child of trauma, especially with RAD or DSED, into any satisfactory conclusion around the irrationality of their decisions. You're nodding your head because you know. You've tried.

SENSE OF POWER

Our kids feel "safe" when they have complete control over everyone around them. This might be through physical bullying, emotional attacks, manipulation of people in their circles, charming strangers and acquaintances to get their needs and wants met, dishonesty, stealing, on and on.

When we respond with anger or frustration to the child's behavior, we support their belief that they are in control and have all the power. This not only leads them to a false sense of security, but inflates their already large sense of power. It might be easy to interpret this dance as a war for control. And while, in some ways, showing your child of trauma that you are indeed in control can alleviate some of the behaviors, this is really a symptom of the greater problem. The problem is that they feel unsafe and distrustful and use control as a weapon.

This is why lying is such a prevalent symptom of children with RAD or DSED. Any truth is vulnerability. It's being real and transparent, even when it's answering simple questions like, "How was your day?" or "What's your favorite food?" Typical kids will lie to stay out of trouble, but kiddos of trauma will lie to not tell the truth, thus resisting opportunities to connect with you.

When I started fostering, I knew the kids would lie over typical things, but lie about a perfectly good day just to avoid the truth? I couldn't wrap my brain around it. But I learned to accept that this was a scary place for my children. So I gave them fewer opportunities to lie. Instead of asking questions, we resorted to simply stating the things we knew were true, avoiding the opportunity to lie, my frustration around being lied to, and their sense of remaining in control because they'd withheld something from us. Conversations generally went better when we didn't ask questions we already had answers to. "What were you thinking?" will never lead to a satisfying response!

It helped me to realize that the lying wasn't just to irk me, but was again, a product of a brain that was flipped around. Terrified. Terrified of losing control and being in a position of helplessness, powerlessness, putting their life at risk. I know many children who struggle with this even into adulthood. Some who, even in their romantic partnerships, present such a false self that their partner really doesn't know them at all. And when anyone begins to get close, the unprocessed trauma caught in their brain is triggered, and they push the person away, making excuses about why their partner was an awful person. It's so much bigger than lying. It's about staying alive.

Interestingly enough, studies have also shown that pathological liars have less gray matter in their prefrontal cortex and more white matter than a typical person.[1] A typical brain has a capacity for lying in the part of the brain also responsible for a person's moral code and feelings of remorse. In a person who lies as a lifestyle, there is a larger capacity for lying, but less inhibition or remorse according to the pathology of their brain. Crazy, right? This is just an example of how behavior is connected to early brain trauma.

Another way sense of power manifests is through a fancy word: triangulation. This basically means that the child sees themselves in a triangle relationship with everyone they know, and they are the orchestrator of the other two points on the triangle. To stay "safe," the child must keep everyone at odds with one another, deflecting from the child's own issues, keeping the attention on someone else.

Man, I've parented some masters of deflection and triangulation. This means that in every relationship, our child will choose someone to buddy up with and someone to target. Who the "buddy" is might change from day to day or event to event, depending on what they are trying to get. They will often "buddy up" with the easiest person to manipulate. They will direct the attention of the buddy to the deficiencies of the "problem." This happens between parents, between therapist and parents, between school and parents, between siblings and parents. Usually one or both parents are "the problem" and anyone else in the vicinity is the buddy. This is like living with Dr. Jekyll and Mr. Hyde. It can make you feel crazy, literally. If you're the targeted parent (most often, but not always, the mother), the child will do everything to present you as the "bad parent." And the other parent will believe it! Because this kid, who's been through so much, is finally *warming up to them*! This must mean they are getting it right, and the other parent still isn't.

This happened in our home. As the Institute for Attachment called it, I was the *Nurturing Enemy*.[2] I was the representation of the first mother who failed this child. And if my child had been in multiple homes, I also represented every "failed" mother before me. And I got the benefit of paying for her mistakes, no matter how great of a mother I was.

This was exceptionally evident in a couple of the children we parented. One particular child would "buddy-buddy" with my husband and whisper about all the bad things I did or said or thought. My husband felt caught in the middle. He was appreciating and enjoying what felt like progress that he had made with our child. At last! A relationship was forming and it felt good. But I wasn't catching on to the game. Our child still treated me with hostility behind my husband's back:

speaking disrespectfully, lying, stealing, sneaking, manipulating, complaining to others about how much I neglected them, didn't feed them, or provide basic needs. (Fortunately, our community was small and we were well-known—and our kids didn't look neglected in any way, because they weren't.)

My husband felt stuck between my frustration and our child's growing "affection" for him. The exhaustion and depletion of raising multiple children with attachment dysfunction kept us hypervigilant, emotionally and physically ALL. THE. TIME. That left very little capacity for us to fight for our marriage. We landed on the couch of a therapist, on the precipice of break up. Neither of us wanted that, but we couldn't see a way out of our pain and struggle. I was drowning and had no support. He was the only other adult living in the house with me to see Mr. Hyde show up, and he was torn between being a source of attachment for our child and supporting me. I lived with the daily strange feeling that he had to choose between us—and that felt weird. This was our kid! Why couldn't he do both? But we were swamped, confused, and *being manipulated*.

During our counseling session, my husband was processing how much he hated being in the middle. The counselor looked him in the eyes and said, "Then stop. Stop being in the middle. Be for your wife. She's not perfect. She's going to make mistakes. But be for *her*." A light bulb went on for both of us. That would be okay? To choose me? But we took this kid in to love and heal, and what if choosing to support me meant losing this child's budding attachment? This brought us face-to-face with some of our own expectations and dysfunction around parenting these kiddos. We'd totally lost sight of "us first" as a marriage.

My husband took it to heart and stopped playing the man-in-the-middle. He continued to show affection and love to our child, but as soon as he wouldn't engage conversation about my shortcomings or mediate between us, our child dropped the "buddy-buddy" game and took a new approach. It was now the community against us, as a unit. And the therapist against us, as a unit. For the first time in our parenting of this child, my husband experienced first-hand what I'd been living with the whole time. It was eye-opening, and it radically changed our marriage and our awareness of how to truly interact with and love this child. Enabling a child's triangulation only supports his or her sense of being in control and of feeling powerful, delaying the healing we *think* is happening with a budding attachment.

For more validation and understanding on this, make sure to read this powerful article from the Institute for Attachment called *How an Adoptive Mom Becomes a Nurturing Enemy: The Unfortunate Effects of Reactive Attachment Disorder.*[3] (I wept the first time I read it, and am so fortunate that my husband saw it, too.) If you think this might be you or your marriage, do yourself the biggest favor and soak up the validation that your experience is real—and just as twisted as it feels.

Present Focus

Everything is now. Consequences to actions, if they don't occur immediately, seem disconnected to our kiddos. And many of these kids are so resilient (which has saved them!) that they only experience the pain of poor choices for a few minutes, if that. Soon, the moment passes, the sting is gone, and they're immediately back to the behavior that brought them pain to begin with. They can seem entirely unaffected by consequences. This is in part because their brains are stuck working primarily from the amygdala, keeping their trauma—and everything—in the very moment. This is also partly because showing you any sign of being affected by your imposed actions on them gives *you* the power, and that's terrifying to them. They cannot let on that you have any influence over them or they have to acknowledge they are not in control, and that means their death. This understanding doesn't mean we don't offer consequences. It simply means they must be immediate, and we can't determine the success of the consequence based on his or her reaction or following choices.

My husband and I learned this the hard way (as we learned nearly everything about parenting children of trauma the hard way). One of the kids we parented owed money to the library. We kept reminding this child to return her book before the deadline. She didn't. And she accrued a fine. A school trip to a theme park was approaching, and we told her she would not attend the school field trip if she didn't find a way to pay off the fine. We thought we'd take the opportunity to help the child learn that when her actions cost money, we weren't going to bail her out financially. We also thought the motivation for the trip would kick this particular booty into gear. But the trip drew closer and closer. I began to panic on the inside. She was going to miss this trip! That wasn't what I wanted. For one, the kid going on the trip would give us a break. Secondly, I love opportunities for my kids to have fun with their friends. I really do! One of my favorite things is sharing life experiences with people I love. And if I can give that joyful gift to my kids—Wow! And now my kid was at risk—for a stupid library fine—of not going.

So being the good behavior analyst that I was, I sat my child down to talk about her goal to attend the trip (I didn't know about the dark prefrontal cortex stuff yet) and how she could reach it. I talked with her about the $2 library bill and ways she could earn that money. She could go next door and offer to mow the lawn. She could sell some toys. She could make lemonade and sell it. Anything! She seemed relatively engaged while we talked. Even walked around our cul-de-sac (though I'm not sure she actually talked with anyone).

The day arrived... and she missed the trip. She was bummed the night before. Bummed the morning of. Our kid was home because it was a school trip and no one was at school.

Being bummed lasted the first half of breakfast. We had the conversation about how two bucks was a lousy reason for missing a super fun trip. And then, she was over it. Bouncing around, laughing, happy as all get out. As if nothing had happened. It was over! The new present moment was a free day at home. No connection to the fun she was missing.

We learned a few things from this experience. One, don't be anxious for your kids. They are more than happy to let you carry the weight of their choices while they go on making them recklessly. I carried the weight of the impending trip for my child. Stressed over it. Tried to help her plan her way out of it. Our kid was perfectly content to let me work the whole thing out for her (and still not take action on it). I wasted a lot of energy stressing about the trip she'd miss and how badly I wanted her to go.

Secondly, we learned not to give consequences that are consequences for us too! A day at home with me was a consequence for me, too. I'm an introvert and relished the quiet days while my kids were at school. I also needed a break from the emotional drain and hypervigilance of parenting our children of trauma. We learned to get creative with our discipline. To still find effective consequences that fit the action, but didn't punish us in the meantime. And sometimes that meant extending "grace" this "one time" (really, though so we could have the space we needed.) "Oh, you're grounded but want to sleep at a friend's house (and give us a break from the crazy)? Hmmm, okay... well, you have done a really great job breathing today. We appreciate that you've (find anything) and we will make this one exception. Have a great time!"

Thirdly, we learned that lectures (or what we thought were highly educational, life-changing conversations) don't go anywhere. The darkened prefrontal cortex takes that info dump and decides to make use of the time strategizing the next attempt at being in control, and thus, safe. Actually, even a healthy PFC doesn't respond well to info dumps. (Read *Wired for Story* to learn more about that!)

DISCONNECTED THINKING

Because they live so much in the present, a child of trauma will often live disconnected from one thought to another, one choice to another, one event to another. They don't naturally make connections. This means that they often don't see how their choices hurt (or help) others or themselves. They don't tend to generalize information.

For example, you told your child not to cross the street without an adult present. The next street they come to, they attempt to cross without an adult. "But I just told you not to cross the street without an adult!" you say. To which he or she responds, "You didn't say *this* street. You said *that* street." This is where, if you're like me, you stand there dumbfounded as your own brain rushes through all the things you will have to say for them to understand every rule ever, unwritten or written, societal, cultural, familial—there's no way. These kids struggle to bridge the idea that not crossing "the" street without an adult means *all* streets without an adult.

Disconnected thinking also shows up in a series of events. A child won't connect cause and effect, or circumstances on a time continuum. It's all now, nothing connected to the second before or the second after. Interestingly, this can also affect their physical sensations. Often our children of trauma have different reactions to touch, temperatures, even emotions than a healthier brain will. They can appear hypersensitive to each of these things or unaffected at all. This is a disconnection of their mind from their bodies. This information alone makes me want to go back to bed. But don't worry! We will cover tips and strategies for addressing these challenges.

If you're a parent raising this kid, you get it. You get the challenges. I hope you're hearing that you're not alone! And that there are valid reasons your parenting and love have not seen the results you thought they would. It's not because you're bad or wrong or a horrible person or parent. It's the opposite actually!

Because you love, this child is in a home. Because you love, their brain has an opportunity to encounter new experiences, pave new pathways, and begin to heal. The healing is slooooooooooow, but can *begin* because you've stuck with it and kept pouring, even when everything seemed to seep out the bottom.

So now that we understand that our kids have come from hard places and their survival response is powerful and real, let's talk about the impact on our families, both positively and negatively. This is the meat of the experience that led me to write *Reclaiming Hope: Overcoming the Challenges of Parenting Foster and Adopted Children.* And I still encourage you to read it for a more focused look on exactly that—how to keep your eyes focused on hope in the dark seasons of the soul. Because parenting children of trauma will take you to the lowest parts of your existence, only to raise you back up again (Lord willing) with a new resilience, a new freedom, a new compassion, and a whole new framework through which to see the world. Keep these words in mind as we transition to the impact the kiddos have on the people around them.

CHAPTER 10

BUT FIRST, SOME VALIDATION

L iving with children (or adults) who have an inability to respond to logic or reason, have a high commitment to their sense of power, are present-only focused, and disconnected in their thinking can be devastating for a family. We have experienced in our own home, and in the homes of families raising children of trauma, just how challenging it can be. (This is why I wrote my first book, *Reclaiming Hope*. We needed hope!)

Let's pause to validate the impact of inviting the manifestation of trauma into your home.

This is not to dissuade you from adopting (if you're thinking about it) or convince you that you made the wrong decision (if you've already done it). Instead, this is to bring validation to your experience. It's time to legitimize what you've been experiencing and ultimately, to lend understanding as to why so many of your efforts seem to fail.

Believing that your love can heal this child is like believing that if you love a child with paraplegia in a wheelchair enough, he or she is going to stand up and start walking. That child *and yours* have physical disabilities preventing your *love* from being the healing element. They need more than love. They need accommodations, re-set expectations, and lots of trauma work so that you can live in more peace together.

This next section is about connecting the dots: recognizing your child in these behaviors and, maybe for the first time, connecting the impact to what causes it. This will not necessarily make your child's behaviors change, but it will help guide your own heart and thoughts around how to have the most healthy home and self possible.

The following chapters will cover how to navigate the impact of our kiddos, how to grow into healthier people while raising them, and how to have hope for their (and our) future.

The next section, Section 2, will address the impact of these disorders, primarily RAD and DSED, on the kids and their families. And finally, in Section 3, we'll look at treatment options for kids (or their parents) dealing with these challenges.

SECTION 2

The children who need love the most will always ask for it in the most unloving ways.

—*Russel Barkley, Ph.D.*

CHAPTER 11

IMPACT ON OUR KIDS WITH ATTACHMENT DISORDER

T he impact of our children's attachment disorder(s) on themselves, we their family, and the general community is widespread. Really, I think we're only beginning to understand the many ripples that stem from our children's behaviors. The people who know the consequences best have all received degrees from SOHK—School of Hard Knocks. That's us! When your family feels attacked from every side, you do your best to figure out what the enemy is and how to conquer it. It feels like survival, and for some, it literally *is* survival.

While the therapeutic community is beginning to awaken to the need for more conversation (and subsequent answers) around attachment disorders, we as parents are leaps and bounds ahead of the game. That's probably not terribly reassuring when, as the parent, you can barely keep your head above water, let alone figure out what all of this means for yesterday and tomorrow. I say all of this as a therapist and as a mama. Within the therapeutic community, I find so many practitioners, my colleagues, who do not understand the attachment disorders we face in the least. I surely didn't. I've had to advocate for my children and our needs, and educate my own professional community to get the help my kids needed, and to be honest—never did get.

This is partly our responsibility. Firstly, we just didn't know what we were up against. Secondly, we moved out of the country with even less opportunity for the help we needed. By the time we realized what true, effective help looked like, it was too late. Not too late for their healing. Not hopeless. But with eighteen-year-olds, the access to care is even more restricted and requires their willful, intentional participation.

I'll talk more about parents later, but for now, let's look at the impact of attachment dysfunction on the kiddos themselves.

I have spent a lot of time with children who have attachment disorders (AD). My own, yes, but also those of friends who are still raising their kiddos, or who've already launched them. And while my personal professional therapy work doesn't treat AD specific kids, I'm on a man-hunt to figure this thing out and help people master it. Lord, have mercy. So the following observations about the impact of AD on our kids are from personal experience, lots of articles I've read, conversations I've shared, and what we scientifically know of the brain.

While we most notably experience the impact on our personal selves, our kids are also deeply impacted by their own AD. Not only are they impacted presently, but as they step into their future as well.

Brené Brown, a well-known researcher (and research professor) is a thought leader on topics like shame, belonging, boundaries, compassion, vulnerability, and more. In her book, *The Gift of Imperfections*, she says,

> After collecting thousands of stories, I'm willing to call this a fact: A deep sense of love and belonging is an irreducible need of all women, men, and children. We are biologically, cognitively, physically, and spiritually wired to love, to be loved, and to belong. When those needs are not met, we don't function as we were meant to. We break. We fall apart. We numb. We ache. We hurt others. We get sick. There are certainly other causes of illness, numbing, and hurt, but the absence of love and belonging will always lead to suffering (Emphasis mine).

Now, a lack of loving, being loved, and belonging lead to all the things she mentioned in a typically functioning person. Catch my drift? Now enter our kids. Wired in every way to need love and belonging, yet fighting against the neurological rewiring of their brain, which prevents them from the very thing they need to survive. It's upside down and backwards. Attachment disorder is cruel.

So here are our kids, with the same desperate need as the rest of us, but with everything stacked against them. Their survival instinct, according to their hijacked amygdala, is to keep everyone at a distance in order to stay safe. But that's not safe! It's suffering. Our kids are caught in a cycle they can't get out of without a lot of help. Their survival behaviors: manipulation, hurting others, sabotaging relationships, and dishonesty to avoid intimacy all work to keep them isolated. Their foster and adoptive placements are often disrupted, families giving notice and passing them on because they cannot meet the needs of these kids, further affirming the brain's lie that people can't be trusted and no one will ever love them. Suffering. And as their behaviors increase to match the growing affirmation of their brain's lie, they increase their chances of preventing love and belonging in their lives.

Our kids are at higher risk of depression, learning difficulties, addiction, low self-esteem, sexual acting out, incarcerations, and passing on AD to their children. Why? Because they are wired for love and belonging, but the very thought of it feels like a death threat. But not having it *is* a death threat. Their behaviors become more disruptive, causing more distance in friendships, family relationships, romantic relationships, until they're alone again and convinced, once more, that they are unworthy of love. They become addicted to chaos, via the adrenaline rush that floods their brain, and to get a fix, push all your buttons. While they blame everyone else, deep down, many of them wonder if it's *them* (especially as they grow into adulthood and the relationship problems are no longer restricted to parents).

The crazy thing is that these kids are surrounded, often, by the most extreme, desperate, selfless kinds of love—and they don't see it. This was reinforced as I read *Boundaries: When to Say Yes, How to Say No, To Take Control of Your Life* recently by Dr. Townsend and Dr. Cloud. It's a worthy read on the importance of having healthy physical, emotional, mental, and spiritual boundaries in life so that we can love well and *be* loved well.

They said,

> "Our basic sense of ourselves, of what is real and true about us, comes from our significant, primary relationships. That's why many people who were unloved in childhood can be inundated by caring people in their adult years, yet not be able to shake a deep sense of being worthless and unlovable, no matter how much people try to show them their lovability."[1]

We see this even in adulthood. Children who were neglected of love in their most important years struggle now and into their adulthood with receiving and experiencing the love all around them.

One holiday, I gave one of my kiddos an album of memories from the previous year. We do this for every kid, no matter how long or short they're a kid in our home. We never wanted our home to be one more stop with no photos, no memories, and a blip along their journey. That year, I gave our kiddo his book. It was during a really rough patch in our experience together. He was in a temporary respite situation and we went to visit him at his respite home over Christmas. He looked through the book. Tears filled his eyes. "Mom," he said, "when I look at this book, I see a kid who was really loved." I smiled, knowing he was seeing the truth. A rare moment. "But how come I've never experienced it?" he asked, looking up at me. I took a deep breath.

"Son, it's true. You've been loved, are loved, and will always be loved. And the reason you haven't been able to experience it is because when you were young and your birth home wasn't very safe, your brain tried to reorganize and figure out how to keep you alive. It did a good job while you lived in that home. But when you moved into a safe home, your brain wasn't convinced. Over the years, in an effort to keep you safe, your brain has fought against you feeling love and belonging. But it's been there the whole time. It's here now." He listened. He took it in. Asked questions. We suggested he talk about it with his therapist, who was also doing research into AD, as a way to keep learning how to help his brain flip back to "normal" since he's now in a safe place.

The conversation was good. A precious and rare moment where we connected, and it felt authentic. He was present. He was raw. And it lasted as long as that conversation. In the following days, he returned to believing that it was everyone else who was against him, he didn't have attachment injury, and he just needed to be free of us. He eventually got what he wanted, but his life didn't change. He doesn't feel any more loved by the world than he did with us. Not from roommates, friends, partners, or birth family members. But I believe it's in there. And he still has the album.

Not only are our kids unable to experience the love many have for them, but in many cases, they become isolated and lonely. Many well-meaning friends and mentors will eventually part ways with our AD kiddos. They can only take so much of the lying, the stealing, the manipulation. One of my children had faithful friends who were determined to help her. The friends weren't entirely aware of the disorder, and often when they were, they didn't believe it. But with time, as things ended up missing from their homes or crazy stories replaced reality, these friends moved on. False allegations keep many caring adults caring from a distance. Our kids are wired for love and belonging but push the salve to their soul, our love, as far away as possible.

I realize this sounds pretty bleak. How will they survive? How can we get our love through their disordered brains? How can we keep the conversation going longer than a few minutes? How will they heal? You have all this love to pour out on them—what do you do with it all? It slides right off like water off a duck's feathers. But they need it.

A book called *When Love is Not Enough: A Guide to Parenting Children with RAD* was recommended to me when we were in the thick of parenting challenges. The title alone seemed to sum up my entire parenting experience with my kids with AD at the time. We had entered fostering and adopting with a sense that our love would be enough to bring healing and wholeness to our kids. That the problem had been the lack of love in their lives up until us. And if we could just saturate their cups to overflowing, they'd bloom and blossom and change the world with their restoration. All we needed was our willing hearts. We brought them in, excited for all we knew they had coming: Disneyland trips, faithful friendships, consistency, reliability, honest parents who could be trusted, music lessons, enough food, first trips to the beach and mountains, birthday parties, hugs and snuggles, and on and on. I imagine our eyes glowed with the visions that passed before us of how we could show our love to these kids.

And we showed it, man did we show it. First, in many of these superficial things. Then, in the laying down of our very selves. Our own mental health, physical health, marriage, and other children—that sacrificial love that lays everything else at the stake to prove to this *one* that they're loved. And then they're still not. When Love is Not Enough. We lived it and breathed it, grieved it, ached over it, and believed it.

Then our kids grew up, and some of them moved out. Moved on. Moved back to birth families, birth communities, and birth dysfunctions. Over a decade of loving and parenting them seemed utterly lost. We literally had nothing but our bruises and scars to show for it... then he called. Reached out. Opened up. She showed up. Talked. Cried. Came home. Not home, like back to our home. But home, to our hearts, with our hearts. When the world beats them down, they come home through a phone call or a text message. I realized, love might just be enough. Just not the enough we thought it was or should be.

What I've learned is that our love was not enough to heal them in our home, or to bring about the dreams we'd had for our relationships with them. Our expectations were too high. We just didn't know. But our love still matters. It isn't lost or wasted. All those years of pouring and pouring filled something. It filled the part of their souls, way deep down, that knows we love them unconditionally. That recognizes that we should have quit, and didn't. Or that we did quit for their good, to get them the help we couldn't offer. Beneath all the injured-brain pieces, right where their souls long for belonging and love, is a quiet cup that's full. All the love that seemed to slide right off? It didn't. A remnant somehow found its way down and settled in that cup. Doing a work in the depths of the soul, sprouting unseen seeds. And even though it's *way* deep in there, when it matters, it matters. And they call. Text. Even dropping a line that I've longed to hear: "Mom, I love you."

The many years of investing and pouring and loving and not giving up created an invisible tether that none of us could see. And that tether is why our kids still call home. It didn't heal in the way we'd expected. Or in the timeframe we had in mind. But the story isn't over, and we have a love-tether that gives us hope that healing may yet come. You might have invisible love-tethers, too.

So don't quit the loving, whatever that looks like for you. Don't totally buy that love isn't enough. It *is* enough, just not as we thought. It's enough for us. And it matters to them. And who knows how many years until that quiet little cup down below rises to the surface, flooding their brains to healing and health—and our kids take a chance at life. Maybe we won't see it with our eyes in our lifetime or theirs, but I still believe it matters. I believe the love you've shown, for whatever length of time you have them, matters. It matters more than we know. It feeds their need and touches their suffering so it's just a little less.

NOT ONLY ARE OUR CHILDREN IMPACTED BY THEIR TRAUMA, BUT THE entire family they come into experiences consequences (positive and negative) as well. This includes you, your spouse, and any other children in the home. It also affects your relationships with extended family, close friends, acquaintances, church communities, and the general neighborhood. Perhaps, like us, you felt relatively equipped to take in a stranger's child, love them like your own, and launch them all nice and rescued into the world, to live out a better possibility than the one they'd been given. Then, upon arriving, they responded to all of your very skilled parenting—in the opposite! That left me, for a short time, entirely flabbergasted and paralyzed. But we rallied, regrouped, researched, and finally found some new tools that seemed to work.

But these tools brought confusion and judgment from many parents of typical children. Why? Because their strategies worked on *their* kids. So, naturally, they knew how to parent kids and we didn't. "Have you tried time-outs?" they'd ask kindly. "What if you just bought tuna in oil instead of tuna in water? That little act of love would probably mean so much to him." Yes, we tried it. We had tried it all. Multiple times. But just for the heck of it, I'll switch tuna types. Did it work? No. The thing the kid agonized over one day simply changed to something different soon enough. Something that prevented them from liking us because liking us is scary.

So in order to practice our new skills, my husband and I faced judgment. (And believe me, I write this paragraph acknowledging my own previous criticism of parents who had unruly children. I know, I'm so sorry, world.)

The thing about parenting children with attachment dysfunction is: It's taxing. It takes a toll on us physically, emotionally, mentally, in all the ways you can think of. The above simple example of tuna, if you're parenting one of these kiddos, is a can of more than tuna! It's the exhaustion of dealing with suggestions from well-meaning people that you've tried ad nauseam without success. It's the reminder that others around you think if you just do this one more thing, your kid will feel loved. It's the reminder that your child doesn't feel loved. That maybe you failed, are a failure, or made a mistake. It's the actual energy required to have these conversations every day. It's the disappointment that another friend, or family member, or therapist still doesn't get it. Or believe you. Or both. That you are truly alone in the world. It's the anger and injustice over how hard you've tried, how much you've poured, how many other "tunas" you've bought. And after all that, you're frustrated to still be in this place. It's not just tuna, folks. It's your physical, emotional, and mental energy zapped, threatening to leave only a shell of you in its wake. You'll probably buy the tuna because what if it really *is* this one dumb thing and it will all get better. Or because that's what loving parents do. Or because you want your friend/family/therapist to know you're not too high and mighty to try their idea. Knowing all the while that it won't work.

The next chapters are my call to you to take care of yourself. Love does not mean driving yourself or your marriage to an early grave. You're no good to anyone there. So let's be super mindful about the ways we can be impacted, and then work toward reducing the negative impact and increasing the positive. Follow me into the next few chapters where we will talk about the physical, mental, and emotional impact we experience raising our children.

CHAPTER 12

IMPACT ON US: PHYSICAL

Spending significant time with children of trauma can have a variety of effects on a person. You know it personally. You were nodding your head when I listed the behaviors earlier. You know the day in and day out of chasing after these kids. The hypervigilance of making sure everyone is safe. That they're safe. That the other children are safe. The constant pull on your attention to know all things at all times. It's exhausting. And when you're exhausted, you are way less likely to make healthy meals and do all of your regular workouts. It's all you can do to get to bed, which still might be light and restless because who knows what's going down in your house while you're sleeping (we've got some stories if you need any ideas). It's almost like being a mother to a newborn... except it never ends. Ever. And when they're finally off to school and you've got a break, the phone rings. Or your inbox dings. Or someone stops you in the grocery store. And their "quick chat" makes your heart race, stealing not only your physical break from the crazy but now your emotional and mental space too.

Too many days of this, and exhaustion can turn into many things. It can turn into numbing behaviors. I've checked out so many times, in so many different ways. Some seemed healthier and others were clearly just junk for the soul. I've used Netflix shows, YouTube channels, Facebook, print books, sleep, and Christian podcasts (because they seem safe and holy) to numb the pain I felt. Some days, the pain was SO big that not even the world wide web could numb it enough to make it better.

Some parents might resort to bigger numbing agents: alcohol, legal drugs (or illegal), gambling, pornography. For an adoptive parent who has struggled with numbing behaviors in the past, the risk is great that the pressures you're facing raising children with AD may trigger feelings you thought you'd overcome. Be mindful of this and have a support network and accountability to keep you on track. Numbing behaviors suck us into a time warp, temporarily promising reprieve from the struggle, but really only adding to it. It keeps us disconnected from loved ones in the home as well as healthier tasks that might support us instead.

If you're finding yourself drawn toward a numbing behavior, be intentional about choosing something more productive, like going for a walk alone or with a friend. Sign up for a dance class. Take a music or art lesson so you can turn to your new hobby when you need a break. Set up regular times of retreat or respite to regroup. It's not needing a break from the fatigue and craze that's bad, it's how we respond to that urge that either supports us or doesn't.

I've also known many parents (me and my husband included) who have ended up dealing with heart palpitations as a physical response to the stress. I have a relatively harmless heart disorder, Premature Ventricular Contractions (PVC), which is exacerbated by caffeine, alcohol, and yes, stress. I can easily reduce the first two, but stress lives in my house. Therefore, we must get creative in addressing the stress.

If we're not finding outlets, like the ones I mentioned above, we will likely find our bodies manifesting the stress physically. For me, that means a heart that begins to beat uncomfortably and frequently. (I have even taken myself to the hospital just to make sure that what I was experiencing was my normal heart condition versus slowly dying.) I have another friend whose heart will race too fast, too long. Another friend's heart seems to skip beats, taking his breath away momentarily. Definitely check with your doctor if you are facing these symptoms. And make sure to tell them about the stress you live with. Consider ways to bring down your stress levels. For example, I recently read an article that just 45 minutes a day of creating, whether it's collage or clay or painting, reduces the cortisol in our system.[1]

Which brings me to cortisol—my physical nemesis after too many years of high stress. Cortisol is a hormone that your body releases in response to stress. According to WebMD, cortisol is produced in the Adrenal glands at the top of your kidneys.[2] Really, cortisol was designed by your body as part of an alarm system. When you're in danger, your adrenal glands produce cortisol to help fuel your body's Fight-Flight-Freeze response (we talked about this in earlier chapters). In life-threatening situations, cortisol is our best friend. However, when our hypothalamus decides that we don't have enough cortisol in our system to combat the never-ending stress of raising our kids with AD, and adjusts the amount all the time, parts of our body begin to weaken. For example, cortisol can change or shut down your immune system, your reproductive system (ladies, ever notice a change in your period around times of stress?), your digestive system, and even growth processes (think of children whose growth is stunted by malnutrition, yes, and chronic stress).

When we have too much cortisol in the system for too long, our body begins to weary. We begin to experience anxiety or depression. We might get headaches or have problems with our memory or concentration. We might develop heart disease! We will have trouble sleeping and, we will likely deal with weight gain. Cortisol loves to hang on to fat. It changes your cravings to sugary, fatty things in response to the higher insulin levels. It's also convinced that you're burning a bunch of calories trying to save your life, and leads you to eat more. It simultaneously slows down digestion (thus metabolism). And we all know that with unhealthy weight gain, other health problems join the party.

Clearly, the effects of chronic stress, which we face daily in raising our kiddos, is slowly killing us. I'm not being dramatic. Left to its own discourse, we will slip into a very dangerous cycle of depression, very poor health, and sleep our lives away if we don't address the physical manifestations of our unreleased stress.

So how do we reduce chronic stress and too-high levels of cortisol in our bodies?

1. Do your best to sleep well. If your numbing behaviors are like mine, they can suck hours of your life. And when you should be working on sleeping, you're staring at a screen instead (which has actually been shown to cause worse sleep once you get it).[3] Turn off the screens and go to bed! Try to find your minimum for sufficiently feeling rest and be committed to getting it.

2. Build in some level of physical activity. I know we're exhausted and busy, but do it. And don't pressure yourself to do something intense! The reality is "stressing" your body in exercise can actually increase your cortisol temporarily. Mild or moderate exercise doesn't normally increase cortisol but helps your body process everything that's "stuck" in the system, while decreasing cortisol later.

3. Know Thyself. Pay attention to what causes your stress. Be aware of your triggers and antecedents. That is, know what happens just before you're triggered, then implement your strategy for addressing it. For example, a couple of the kids I've parented are especially hurtful. They know the buttons to push and they attack my value as a mom. I'm often blindsided by the subtle attacks (How? I have no idea. You think I'd be a master ninja pro at heading these off). So now I know that when said child is around, I need to have music playing. And not just any music, but music pre-chosen and part of a playlist to speak directly to my value. So whatever happens, I've been filling my mind before, during, and after any encounters with truth and affirmation, making the attacks of my child less likely to get in. Maybe this isn't your thing, but *have a thing*. Maybe you choose to use breathing exercises. Journaling. Monitoring your heart rate and having a plan for regulating it. Speaking of music, even if this isn't your specific jam, music has also been shown in studies to reduce stress. Find something that calms you, speaks to you, and play it often. (To enjoy my playlist, see the Resources at the end of the book).

4. Get Away. Utilize respite. Don't have any? Make it a priority. Getting away and regrouping is SO important. Are they worse when you get back? No worries. Getting away for some refreshing and coming back to the craze does suck, but it's way better with bubbles of refreshment in between. And when you get away, have fun. Do something to distract yourself while building into friendships or family members who need the break as much as you do. While you're at it, find a reason to laugh. And do lots of it. Laughter decreases cortisol, too! I love reading websites about autocorrect fails. (I usually laugh so hard I'm suffocating and crying at the same time... makes for a good calorie burn on top of it just feeling really good!)

5. Keep community. One day, a sweet friend who, by all external appearances, had the perfect children came up to me. "Marcy, your kids came up to me today and I just wanted to punch them in the face." I cried. I really did. Not because I wanted people to punch my children. But because she got it. She loved me, she trusted me, she believed me, and she hurt for me. Her story looked nothing like mine, but she *believed* me. And in her belief, she wanted to punch my kids (but gratefully didn't). It was a pivotal moment on that sidewalk for me. I realized that friends could support me, regardless of their own life experiences. It wasn't impossible. And in fact, I had a rich, precious group of women that year who surrounded me with such care, such belief, such companionship that it buoyed my spirits to sustain me through the trials that peaked in that season.

Sometimes the impact of raising our kiddos means we will lose friendships and relationships. And sometimes, the impact is a rich group of people who help to hold your head above water. These hardships can both deepen the beauty that's around us and sift the frauds from among us. I'm grateful for that group of ladies, among whom I was the only adopted mama. But each one had a story that needed a believing friend to come along and offer a shoulder, some chicken salad, and Kleenex. Get a group of them for yourself.

6. Know someone with a pet? Pet sit. Or get one yourself. Animals are such incredible therapy and have literally been shown to reduce stress in humans. (Actually, studies have shown stress levels reduce for the

pets themselves, too, after loving interactions with their humans!)[4] There are so many benefits to having a pet. We see them used in retirement homes as companions for the lonely. We see them visit hospital beds as a salve for the sick or injured. They have a calming effect. Utilize that, even if it's just visiting a pet store or a friend's pet.

7. Connect with your higher power. For me, this means praying to God, being in His Word, and trusting that what He says is true! Knowing that He is sovereign, that He loves me, that He equips me and aids me has kept me going so many times. Studies have also shown a notable decrease of stress among praying people and also among church attendees.[5] Not only is there a positive correlation between prayer and stress, but hey, if there's a God and He's real and He answers prayer— well, why not connect with Him and get some help!

We won't have much control over the circumstances causing us stress right now. But we can do any number of the things mentioned here to reduce our stress levels, reconnect with our physical health and healing, and refuse the detrimental impact of raising our children of trauma on our physical health.

In the next chapters we will cover the impact on our emotional and mental health, along with ways to reduce impact along the way.

CHAPTER 13

IMPACT ON US: MENTAL

N ot only do we face the physical manifestation of our own stress, but we experience it mentally and emotionally as well. For this book's purpose, I will distinguish these two from each other. By emotional, I mean our positive psychological functioning. Can you express emotions appropriately for your stage of life and given circumstances? Do you find yourself overreacting to circumstances in your life? Are you able to gauge what you're feeling, thinking, or how you're behaving, and manage appropriate responses? This is emotional health. Mental health, on the other hand, is concerned with your cognitive thinking. How does your brain process information, store memories, and understand the information it's processing? Mental health includes emotional, social, and psychological well-being. It's from this function of health that we either develop mental illness or we don't.

This chapter focuses on the potential mental impacts when raising children with AD.

We all bring our own stuff to each relationship in life. We carry with us a set of luggage and every time we make a new friend, take on a new partner, birth a child, we invite them to unpack our luggage. And likewise, we're invited to unpack theirs as well. Depending on our level of health, self-awareness, and progress in healing at the time, this can be a positive experience or a negative one. For example, if I'm still working through my own abandonment issues (or am in denial of them) when a friend decides to move across the country, I'm going to unpack my baggage and make up a story that she doesn't really love me, I'm not valuable to her, and I must be unworthy of love and friendship. If I've made some good progress in my abandonment story and recognize my patterns and limiting beliefs, when this friend moves across the country, I will be able to wish her well, hug her big, and know that my value isn't derived from her move. Will it still feel like loss? Yes. Will I be tempted to return to old ways of thinking? Of course. But through practice and discipline I'll be equipped to repack my luggage in a tidier way.

This is the same when we move children into our home. They come with visible luggage, often bound up in a trash bag, and a whole host of invisible luggage. And as they begin to unpack their visible and invisible luggage, we begin to show ours off too.

This is especially true in spaces where we haven't worked through our own abandonment stories. Or through our own stories of shame or worth. For many of my parenting years, I didn't realize that I "needed" my children to demonstrate my worth as a mother. If I got good feedback from them, I was a good mom. If I didn't, I was a failure. My identity as a mother rode on the backs of children of trauma and imperfect bio kids alike. Messy, in process, brains in development, yet I had given them the power to determine my worth. And for a child with AD especially, this is a disaster. Their own dysfunction thrives on the power someone else gives them. I inadvertently created an unhealthy relationship with my kids when I subconsciously determined that they'd be the source of my grade as a mom. This was demonstrated in my feeling intimidated around some of my kids, especially the ones who were quick to tell me how awful I was (through their smirks and snide comments). When I'd bravely own my role as mom, I found myself "paying" for it through silent treatment or a cold shoulder. Sometimes I resisted parenting the child to stay out of "trouble" or avoid retaliation. What an upside-down doozy! As this entered my awareness, I began to process it, talking about it with counselors and close friends. I prayed about it. I read about it. And still I couldn't stop the feelings.

One morning I woke up and it just hit me like a brick: I'M A GOOD MOM. That both feels arrogant and terribly freeing all at once. I'm a good mom! I'm not perfect (and perfect isn't good anyway because who can relate to that?) But I *am* good. I took the children of strangers into my nest and made them my own babies, complete with all the love. I nurtured them, raised them, corrected them, celebrated them, advocated for them, and listened to them. And while I made many mistakes, I also modeled apology and forgiveness seeking. How to handle when one makes a mistake. No one else was in line to mother my kids. *No one.* But I showed up. I'm a good mom.

I needed this new story in my heart. I believe God settled this banner over me so I could begin loving my children with more freedom than ever before. Being a good mom no longer relied on what my kids thought about my decision. Or how much silent treatment I received for making it. It didn't dim the reality one bit that they had an adoring mother who would fight to the end for them, even if they were never able to experience it. My years of looking for approval from them revealed much more about *me*. My deep insecurities. My smallness in my own mind. My fear of my own inadequacy. My lifelong journey to find acceptance and love from others. That was the luggage I'd strewn all over our home. My kids had to walk through it every day for a little while. But that morning, I packed it all back up and tossed it in the dumpster.

It'd be easy to read this and think, "Why the heck was she adopting kids? What a mess!" And it's a fair question. But if we're only looking for the not-messy people to adopt kids, who's left? We all bring stuff to these relationships. And their stuff and our stuff all become a *lot* of stuff. I joked in one of my breakout sessions recently that we needed to KonMari our metaphorical clutter. To keep what sparks joy and put everything else in its place. Mind you, it's metaphorical. If we take this literally, on a bad day, the kids are gone, the veggies are gone, the scale is gone. That's not what I'm talking about.

I'm talking about what gives you joy and keeping that forefront. Personally, as I researched the truth of joy versus momentary happiness, I found that joy is a deep, abiding sense of contentment no matter the circumstances. And in my personal journey, that joy is not only supernatural, but only found in a supernatural source: God. Verse after verse in the Bible describes our joy coming from God's comfort, from thanksgiving, from a faith community, from His help and presence, and even from the growth we experience in trials. This is what we keep when we look at all the clutter. The supernatural joy that chases out the shadows.

And how do we put everything else in its place? With healthy boundaries. Wise counsel. Therapeutic support to process our own baggage and the ways it trips us up. Friends who get it. Journaling. Celebrating every little win! Creative outlets. Redefined expectations. And connection to God. All of these things hold us accountable to our journey. They cause us to take a level of responsibility for what is ours to own and puts it in its place. With all our issues addressed or in progress, we can parent from a much healthier place and focus on helping our kids unpack their luggage, putting everything in its place.

COMPASSION FATIGUE

Sometimes, even with all our own "luggage" nice and sorted, we can begin to experience strange symptoms of our own. We find ourselves wanting to be alone more often, crying easily, or overreacting to small things with too much anger. This is when your caring for someone has slipped into Compassion Fatigue. This can occur when you hear a child's story of trauma and pain and it hits you hard. The pain of what they experienced takes your breath away. You hold it together for them (or you try to), but you are internally broken and outraged at the things they've suffered. It settles on your soul and weighs you down. You can almost hear the sounds and feel the physical pain that your child experienced. That weightiness turns into chronic tiredness, headaches, sadness, difficulty concentrating, nightmares, or feelings of overwhelm or helplessness. And while it might make perfect sense to see the list here, in correlation with caring so deeply for someone's pain, the reality is that when we're in it, we often totally miss it. In fact, one of the major symptoms of Compassion Fatigue is denial!

If you love your child, have experienced some of these things, but are positive this isn't you, it probably is. And it's okay. There's nothing wrong with loving so much that it sometimes hurts. However, there *is* something wrong with not acknowledging it and taking proactive steps to care for yourself so you can care for your child well. Still not convinced? Take this Professional Quality of Life Questionnaire, developed by Dr. Beth Hundall Stamm, one of the world's leading experts on Compassion Fatigue.[1] This assessment will also rate you on a level of Secondary Traumatic Stress (in the following paragraphs) and Burnout.

Should you recognize that you're dealing with a level of Compassion Fatigue, then congratulations! You've taken the very first step toward relieving the burden: acknowledging what you're dealing with. This is so important! That's why it's the first step of Alcoholics Anonymous. Our progress toward any level of health starts with acknowledging our problem.

Next, find someone to talk to. Having other parents who understand is such a breath of fresh air. Or find a therapist who you can talk to and process things with for an hour, someone who won't try to fix it, yet is trained to guide you into healthy thinking and healing.

Work on healthy boundaries. You have the ability to determine what comes in and what goes out of your heart and mind. Be aware of your capacity and be disciplined to contain it within healthy boundaries. This might mean knowing that if a hard conversation is coming up with your child, you will have a friend, therapist, or partner available to process the conversation with later. Or removing yourself from certain conversations and getting a synopsis later. It might mean putting boundaries around the way you receive information. Personally, I have to avoid certain news sites because they share predominately devastating events from around the world. I begin to feel heavy and burdened when I watch them, wanting to sleep off the helpless I feel— helpless to affect change in all the pain our world is feeling, but know I can't. I have to either have a plan for how to lift myself up after viewing the news, have a friend around to process it with, or avoid it all together. Think about what this looks like for you, and begin to close the gates to your mind and heart.

Be grateful! Even though your child has experienced an incredible amount of hard or trauma, they are now with you! A good parent. A loving parent. What a gift that you get to love this child. While you would never have asked for them to endure pain so you could be their mom or dad, here they are, and you are a gift to them and vice versa. Find many reasons in your life to be grateful, especially when you're feeling overwhelmed with caring.

SECONDARY TRAUMATIC STRESS (STS)

If Compassion Fatigue isn't addressed, it can easily turn into Secondary Traumatic Stress. Secondary Trauma can come in two ways. First, it can develop as you are exposed to people who have experienced direct or primary trauma and you connect with their pain in a way that begins to affect your quality of life or normal functioning. Second, it can develop when you are exposed to people who've experienced trauma, and the act of providing the care they need leads to a kind of burnout. Your own energy—emotional, physical, and spiritual—that is required to meet their needs depletes you and leaves you feeling helpless and empty. Yet, even on empty, your child's needs remain high and you have to keep giving.

When you give from a place of emptiness, you will expire. I know I expired. At least, that's how my therapist put it. Our survival skills all have an expiration date. Mine was to keep giving, keep giving, keep giving, because that's what I knew to do. What I didn't know to do was to ask for more help. Or recognize the path of destruction I was on. It took everything I had to keep my head above water. But one day, I began sinking and couldn't do it anymore. I found it nearly impossible to stay awake. The smallest activity seemed to sap all of my energy and knock me down for hours at a time. I felt numb, discouraged, frustrated, and more than anything, desperate to have the energy I needed for my children with AD when they got home from school. My whole day was spent building up my capacity and fortitude so I could be on top of those kids. And not just present *for* them, but protecting my household *from* them. Their behaviors often left me feeling afraid to leave anyone alone with them unsupervised. I couldn't need a nap while they were home; who knew what would happen! Most of the time, I knew we'd be having a conversation around the phone call or email or conversation I received that day about their behavior.

One day I found myself in a doctor's office. I was sure there was a problem with my thyroid that they kept missing during my physicals. I needed help. I couldn't stay awake, and I still had younger children at home. "Really," I told my doctor in Germany, "I just need to be rested and awake for when my kids get home. They're really hard and I need to be able to manage my life when they get home." My six-year-old daughter was in a princess dress and rain boots. I don't remember what I had on, but I'm sure I was a mess. Then I became a crying mess. (Children being dressed inappropriately and tears were no-nos in this culture of my heart.) Even so, the sweet doctor saw exactly what was going on.

"Marcy, you are a good mom. And you need a little bridge over this time in your life." She knew I was dealing with STS. She prescribed me some medicine to help me "bridge" this hard season. And amazingly, it worked. It helped me function. Suddenly, I could think clearly again, stay awake when needed, and keep a level head with my kids. Not everyone dealing with STS needs medication. But some do. I did. And I'm not a big fan of meds (unless someone else needs them). But I'm so grateful my doctor knew how to help me. It really was just a bridge, and a year or so later, I was able to maintain healthy functioning on my own. This was eye-opening. It showed the impact of mothering my children with AD on my own brain chemistry. Medicine can't fix what isn't broken. My brain was both over- and under-producing important chemicals for healthy functioning as a result of my own trauma experience.

How was this possible, you ask? In addition to medication, I began personal and marital counseling, found a rich group of friends, joined an online support group for parents of kids with Reactive Attachment Disorder, made a playlist of music to help with my emotions, began implementing healthy boundaries around how much of my emotional energy I'd give to these kids, started using a meditation app called Abide, and with the support of my husband made some important shifts in our home and family dynamics. It wasn't the medicine alone that helped (Though, it was certainly amazing! Why had I waited so long?) but a collaboration of efforts to bring me back up to healthy functioning.

I've still never returned to my original 100%, but I now have a very healthy awareness of my capacity and my responsibility to operate from within it, regardless of the demands around me. If any of my story is resonating with you, get some help. Really, I waited too long. I'm a counselor, and I totally missed it in my own life! I really thought I had some iron deficiency or something else going on. There are many ways that STS presents, not only in fatigue, but if you find yourself struggling to function in any way, reach out for help sooner rather than later. Join a support group. Meet with your doctor to rule out medical needs. Get a good therapist for a time. Bridge this season of your life with the support you need to regain healthy functioning. If you'd like to know more about STS, I cover it in great detail in my book *Reclaiming Hope.*

PRIMARY TRAUMA

Sometimes our exposure to children of trauma leads to direct trauma in our own lives. The ways our children manifest the brokenness of their experiences often causes ongoing traumatic events in the homes of their families. This is a move beyond vicarious or STS, where you're primarily affected because of your burnout on caring. This is actual first-hand trauma in response to your children. I know, it sounds crazy.

Kids can traumatize us? Yes! Not because they intend to, but because their survival skills are so harmful that we get obliterated in the wake of their actions. Some parents have been hit, kicked, spit on, cussed out, threatened, punched, accused, and degraded. For some families, Child Protective Services has come out to respond to false allegations, which can feel terrifying!

We've been judged and condemned. Ostracized. Isolated. Cue the triggers for trauma: helplessness and threat to life. Both are often present when we are raising children with AD. We can't keep *ourselves* safe, our kids with AD safe, the other kids in the home safe, the neighbors safe, the classmates safe... No one. And when we ourselves get stuck in the Freeze cycle, we begin to operate from the same hijacked amygdala as our kids. And remember, this is not where our best thinking or decision-making happens.

Yet it's real. It's so real. I honestly didn't realize the full extent to which we were living in trauma until we had no more kids with AD living in our house. The door would open and suddenly I'd experience the physical response I'd been dealing with for years but had never recognized—a quickened heart rate, a cold sweat, and hypervigilance. And then suddenly, I'd realize that all of this was happening in my body and that I no longer had to be afraid of what would happen once the door closed. This is actually where direct trauma becomes Complex PTSD, which I'll talk about next.

Suffice it to say, sometimes our experiences with the children we love is so extreme we don't even realize the ways we are getting stuck in trauma. Everything I did to deal with STS was effective here as well:

- Having therapeutic support to help me process through the trauma so it could move out of my amygdala and into a healthy part of my brain so I could function from my frontal cortex.
- Playing music that calmed me and reminded me of my identity.
- Friends who listened.
- Online support groups where parents shared my same story but with different names in different homes.

- I also took a course on trauma (and specifically, helping others heal from it). This became as beneficial to my own personal journey as it is to anyone I work with therapeutically. Find someone who has training in trauma and get their assistance in healing.

All of this began to heal the parts of my experience that had become traumatic for me. It wasn't until my kids with AD were gone from the home that I felt space to really do healing work. This is partly because it's hard to heal from trauma when the source of it still lives in your home, recreating it all the time. Now with some time and distance, I've been able to do some good work without all the backward motion of previous years. I'm not saying you can't do some good healing work while they're in your house. Only that it's considerably easier when they're gone. I'm still in a relationship with my kids and we're all still working toward healthy attachment. And even with the distance and time, we still sometimes trigger one another back into uncomfortable places. But my capacity has returned and I'm less phased by their behaviors.

Complex Post Traumatic Stress Disorder

We talked about C-PTSD in Chapter 5. If you remember, it's similar to traditional Post Traumatic Stress, except that its cause is long-term, ongoing exposure to traumatic events. It's exactly what you "married" when you brought a child of trauma into your home with an attachment disorder that manifests as recreating trauma, to be experienced daily by you. C-PTSD is talked about a good deal in connection with children who've been in abusive homes, or spouses who've lived in abusive homes, but very little around the parents who are raising our children.

Let me remind you what to look for with C-PTSD: You might find yourself (or your spouse) experiencing:

- chronic fatigue,

- avoiding others and having difficulty with relationships,
- thinking about death often (not necessarily suicidal, but invasive, frequent thoughts of death),
- negative self-concept,
- and the more typical flashbacks, nightmares, and emotional triggers that manifest physically, such as nervousness, increased heart rate, nausea, etc.

People with C-PTSD may find it difficult to keep attention, concentrate, or stay present. They may find they are responding to situations in an exaggerated way. You might also be dealing with self-blame, guilt, and confusion around the ongoing trauma, even to the point of believing you were somehow responsible for it.

I knew I experienced STS at this point, but genuinely didn't realize that I was also experiencing C-PTSD until I was in it. One of the kids we'd parented had moved on and taken the trauma and all of its manifestations with him or her. We were relieved. We loved this kid so much, but it was time to make space for healing for all of us. The day-in and day-out of dealing with the symptoms of an attachment disorder were like drowning—nonstop.

Finally, we could breathe. We could kick our heads to the surface and breathe deep from the life-giving air. I drove back from the drop-off and felt as though someone had removed a literal weight from my body. I wept the whole drive, overwhelmed by the lightness I felt. Overwhelmed by the light breaking through the clouds. I was overwhelmed with gratitude that we'd made it this far with this kid-turned-adult. We'd made it.

My relationship with kids I've parented has been strengthened by time and distance because 1) I'm not the immediate trigger for their AD anymore and 2) I have enough day-to-day restoration and healing that I have regained capacity and strength to engage them deeply when I do. I'm also not directly affected by their life decisions, nor are the other family members still at home, so I have much more space for empathy, compassion, and kindness. When I hang up the phone after talking my kiddos through life challenges, I'm still in the safety of my own home. All I can do is keep calling, keep reaching, keep loving, and especially, keep praying for their healing. My heart breaks to see their choices and to watch them live the consequences. Just as it broke by bearing the weight of those consequences personally and watching my other children bear them as well.

What I didn't expect was, amidst the relief and celebration of a new start for each of us, a lingering shadow lurking in the corners. The front door opening and closing around dinner time sent my heart racing. A midday phone call took my breath away. Picking apples at the grocery store during the lunch hour put me on high alert. What the heck? I began to notice how much my body had been physically responding to the trauma in my daily life. Except with the source of the trauma removed, my body continued to respond to the associations it held with it. This was so eye-opening. No wonder I couldn't lose the weight I'd gained. No wonder I was still fatigued. My body was constantly on high alert, all the time. And was still, frustratingly, on high alert!

I knew about PTSD and wondered if this is what I was experiencing. I made an appointment with my own therapist and began to process these experiences. She helped me to name it C-PTSD, understand the difference, and then begin healing. We did a lot of breathing work, helping me to return to an awareness of my body and paying attention to life-giving breath. I began to use an app called Abide for guided Biblical meditations and breathing work (link available in "Resources"). We talked through the fears. Together, we moved my traumatic experiences from being stuck in my amygdala back into the normal flow of healthy brain functioning. While I still have sporadic nightmares or heart palpitations around certain interactions, I've done good work in addressing the way raising my children has surprisingly affected my own psyche in a big way.

This is no joke. Some parents walk away unscathed, some with livable symptoms addressed by specialized, temporary therapy, and others need much more intensive care and possibly medication. It's okay. Whatever your needs are to address C-PTSD, do it. And just like all of the other areas of impact, make sure to have good community around you. Join support groups. I've joined a Facebook support group for parents whose children with RAD are now out of the home. It's specific to those of us launching our kids and now living out the C-PTSD in their wake. It's been an amazing group. Find one online or locally. If your kids are still at home and you're dealing with direct and Secondary Trauma, be aware that you'll probably have some C-PTSD once your kids leave. And be prepared to address it. Already have supports in place to help you unravel the years of loving and pouring and drowning.

I have advocated for years now for more conversation around Secondary Trauma and Compassion Fatigue as it relates to adoptive families because no one was talking about it. Or at least, the discussions only addressed social workers and therapists. The people who spend an hour a week with our kids at the *most*. We do the day in and the day out. If anyone needs a conversation around Secondary Trauma and C-PTSD, it's us. The parents raising the kids. So let's keep talking. Let's keep sharing our stories. I know I want to be a genuine help and support to my kids. But like the over-used, but highly relevant, oxygen mask metaphor, we have to help ourselves before we can help our kids. We have to get the System to recognize it is slowly burning bridges and killing families by not supporting us. Adoptions disrupt over these things. Kids remain in the system for these reasons. Until they're willing to help us, and until we realize we need help, our families are going to be individually recreating the wheel in forming healthy adoptive families. And that wheel, if left *only* up to us, will be misaligned, warbled, and weak. We need each other to keep our families together.

Now that we've taken a look at the impact of raising kids with attachment disorder on our physical and mental states, we are going to talk about the impact on our emotional health.

CHAPTER 14

IMPACT ON US: EMOTIONAL

The physical impact of raising kids with AD is relatively easy to notice. We feel it in our bodies. If you're like me, you may not recognize your emotional duress until it's manifested in a cold sore or a kink in your neck or back, or a cold. Our bodies respond to our emotions. In a culture that is so bent on numbing as a coping strategy, we've become very physically sick. We understand physical impact. But we don't always catch the emotional impact. We just keep showing up, doing life, trying to survive, trying to feel as little pain as possible, until we're *in* pain. And this is our culture *without* raising children with AD! Now add the stress of AD to our lives, and we need a whole new level of awareness around our physical, mental, and emotional health.

Being aware of our emotional health is probably one of the most important (though I would personally put spiritual health at the very top— it feeds directly into the other three). When we can understand the emotional impact of raising our children, we can have a strong influence on our own mental and physical health. The two previous chapters are greatly minimized when we address this one.

The emotional impact we experience comes from a variety of places. Our friendships and family relationships are impacted. Our fears rise up and threaten to become reality. Our doubts about our own worthiness, sufficiency, and lovability become real. We experience isolation and embarrassment. To protect ourselves, we become hypervigilant. Our anxiety and stress levels increase. And our reputation is put on the line. Basically, raising children with AD impacts every area of our lives. Let's look at a few of these areas more closely.

FRIENDSHIPS AND FAMILY RELATIONSHIPS

Not only do we have to unlearn parenting and re-learn it for our kids with AD, but we have to do it with strained relationships, when what we need most is community. Our story of the chaos in our home gets old for our friends and family. We start to sound like whiners and complainers. When really, we're drowning and need a life raft *fast*. Some of our friends and family just do not get it. They don't see it (sweet charmers that our kids are), and they don't believe it. They don't trust us; they judge us.

I had some friends who seemed to burn out on the hard. They tried for a long time, but my story was just too different. If only I would "realize this" or "try that" or "recognize this other thing." Surely, my home could be as peaceful as theirs. When I shared vulnerably about the trauma happening in my home, it was somehow my fault. My lack of love or my lack of parenting skill or my lack of understanding. I started to believe that unless someone was literally walking in my shoes or living in my house or heart, they just couldn't understand. I felt alone and isolated. Part of that was because of how few people understand what we actually experience at home. And part of it was self-imposed. Sharing my kids with the world opened us up to more possible judgment, accusation, and misunderstanding.

Many families are just like me, finding it hard to want to go in public with our kiddos. While we need to run typical errands and have healthy connections with people, too many of us have lost friends and family members because of the extreme behaviors of our children and our upside-down-looking parenting. So we begin to crawl into our cave where it's chaotic, protected from the world's judgments, but adds to our own isolation—the very last thing we need to be able to thrive in parenting these kids.

We also had family members who didn't understand or, through their own life experiences and knowledge, decided our challenges were due to personality differences or poor parenting skills. Some of our friends have even had family members cut them off, unwilling and unable to believe that the child has an actual disorder that's causing hardship.

And how could they? Our kids are charming as all get-out with others, and yet turn into "terrors" at home, behind closed doors. Our kids are masters of manipulation, charm, and deception.

But if your family members were to take your kids for a length of time, as ours did, they would likely come around. If your child truly has an attachment disorder, it doesn't go away when living with other people. It will always come out. We've watched this in the lives of our adult children as well. The patterns of their lives are the same, even though we're no longer the ones causing all their problems. The relationship pattern they had with us emerges in every relationship they form— after a brief honeymoon, of course.

One of our family members took one of our kids for a week. That same family member, previously, was sure that we just had something against this kid. That we were too strict and unfair in our treatment of said child. After one week, this family member said something like, "Wow, I feel like I ran around putting out fires for seven straight days. Here's your kid back." The next time we asked if this family member would like to care for our kid, now an adult, longer term, the answer was born straight from the impact of that week: Nope. There wasn't enough money that could turn that no into a yes.

Another family member took one of the kids we parented for a longer length of time. This family member had some experience with children with developmental delays. This member recognized symptoms of ADD, but not of Reactive Attachment Disorder. Yet, we warned that taking in this adult-child would require strong boundaries, a special kind of "coaching," and a willingness to make hard decisions should the time come. The child moved in. To protect my family member, I won't detail the consequence of that decision, but I'll just say that life has never been the same for that family. And my child has very little contact with them. On the flip side, the family member now fully supports us and we have a stronger relationship from the experience.

After reading all of this, you might think that only people who care for children with AD would ever trust us, understand us, and love us. But during one of the hardest years of my life, God gave me a rich and diverse circle of women. None of these women were walking in my shoes. One had experienced challenges raising teens. A couple had "perfect" families by all appearances. One was learning about an Asperger's diagnosis for their young child. But mostly, they were as different from my parenting experience as possible.

And yet.

These women believed me. They cried with me. They prayed for me. They showed up without judgment. Now, lest you think this means they were passive, they weren't. They called me to account when I was sinking too far below. They reminded me of truth—that my kids don't determine my worth and that God has a plan for my family. Sometimes I forgot and they brought me back. They were hands-on. And it was purely friendship.

Friends, these people exist. These family members exist. They might be rare, but they're out there. Don't give up on humanity because of a few bad experiences. Don't isolate yourself because of the immaturity of some. And be gracious with them as they grow. Keep reaching for the people who get it. And keep being a person who gets it, for families like ours, and families *not* like ours. There are plenty of families I can love who are so different from mine. I can believe their stories, call them to flourish, and show up in every place it matters. We can model what this looks like for our families. Until you find friends like this, connect with counselors, mentors, support groups, and your journal for processing the hard things in safe places.

· · ·

ISOLATION

This distrust in our relationships, and lack of understanding, can lead to other issues as well. For example, kids with AD love to tell whoppers of every kind. But their favorite stories involve neglect and abuse. For some reason, passing on stories of neglect and abuse in a current or previous placement seem to provide them with a touch of compassion and attention that they don't find with other stories. We saw this in kids we parented, too. Additionally, telling the truth is vulnerable. So, to keep people distant, they tell the opposite of the truth. In most cases, this opposite is regarding their care. Many loving families have had Child Protective Services show up at their door in response to a report.

I'm a mandated reporter. I get it. I've seen actual abuse, had to report it at times, and understand how many children have been left in traumatizing situations because adults didn't believe them. In a recent child safety training class I took, the leader shared that the majority of children who've been sexually abused don't report until their thirties![1] *If* they report at all. And the number one reason? The children-turned-adults didn't think anyone would believe them. None of us want to perpetuate that kind of ongoing abuse. Unfortunately, that also means that sometimes loving adoptive families raising kiddos with AD quickly become suspects of abuse. Not because there's actual physical evidence, but because of the stories our kids tell.

I'm in favor of the System doing its due diligence to make sure a child is safe. Sadly, some workers have taken on this role at the expense of a good home with a good family. Additionally, we see articles about how a family had their children removed for not giving one of them a flu shot or for letting them play at the neighborhood playground.[2] It's easy to begin to feel fearful and distrustful of CPS's desire for the truth before it takes a sweeping action against someone. It takes social workers, judges, lawyers, families, and friends to understand the nuances of a child with AD and how to genuinely gauge if their adoptive home is truly a threat or not. Many families have endured crazy hard things to love their kiddos, but the threat that CPS would come and take *all* of their children is enough to disrupt most adoptions.

This raises up a primal fear in us—the safety and protection of our children. The thought that they'd be removed from us against our will is enough to make anyone move to Timbuktu. Healthy parents want to protect their homes and their families. When the danger is from within, this is even more devastating. Whether it's a spouse, a parent, or a child, threats from within rock us right to the core of our DNA. A mom or dad having to choose the good of the group over the individual threat feels like choosing between whether to keep your arm or your leg. They are part of you. You love them. And they're bringing a major threat to the family unit. This is a main reason why families would even consider un-adopting or giving notice on a foster child.

My husband and I cared for children who used allegations of sexual abuse for attention. We had to be very vigilant and accountable in every way should an allegation come *our* way. This is a hard way to live! We knew that this wasn't even a temptation in our home, but should the child decide to make up a story, we wanted to have our bases covered. Fortunately, this teenage girl was only in our home for a month and her allegations were minor (and not sexual). We loved her and grieved for her at the same time. At fifteen, behavior like that would likely keep her from a permanent placement. And it did.

THE NURTURING ENEMY

When those of us who parent kids with AD aren't worried about CPS coming, or friends and family cutting us off, we're dealing with our own internal issues. We bring our own abandonment issues, fears, insecurities, and doubts to this parenting role. This would be enough with typical children: addressing our fear of abandonment when our kids reject us with their behavior, addressing our identity as "good parents" when they fail at school, etc. But when our kids have attachment dysfunction, they target and split us in unique ways. Where a typical child will triangulate to get what they want, our children will triangulate as if their life depends on it. Because they genuinely feel like it does. That means no giving up. This is where the term "The Nurturing Enemy" struck particularly true.

The article I mentioned in Chapter 9, *How an Adoptive Mom Becomes a "Nurturing Enemy"* on the website for the Institute of Attachment, a site I highly recommend visiting regularly, changed my life.[3] Well, not changed as in made my kids less triangulating. But changed as in validated the very life I was living without recognition. We took this into marriage counseling with us and it continued to transform how we operated as individuals, as a married unit, and as parents.

The premise is this: Children have a parent-wound. The original birth parent "failed" them in some way. This might be through their illegal and abusive behavior. This might be because of an inability to bond with their child. It might be due to something that was entirely out of their control, like their own untimely death, debilitating illness, or trauma during birth. Whatever the cause, our children have a primal disappointment that is foundational to how they interact with the world.

This is where the Nurturing Enemy comes in. Here steps a loving, nurturing, well-meaning adult into the hole of this first parent. The hole is *big*. But here we come, with all our love and good intentions. But all they can see is Disappointment, Distrust, and Failure in the position of "Mom" or "Dad." More often than not, our children target mother figures as their Nurturing Enemy. The failure of the first mother is the curse of every mother after. No matter how we love, what we pour, how we show up, we are always paying for the first mother. In the psychosis of our child's brain, We. Are. Enemy. And the more we try to fill that role, the more we convince their brains that we are an enemy of their very life. (This can change, slowly, with lots of informed parenting and therapy. Lots.).

If you come to this relationship, as I did, subconsciously (or consciously) looking for affirmation as a parent, identity of worthiness and lovability, or as some kind of resolution to your own broken relationship, you are setting yourself up for devastation. I wish I'd caught this in my own life sooner.

What I didn't realize, when I began parenting over a decade ago, was how much I longed to be liked. In this last year, I've learned that I'm a

9 on the Enneagram. (A great book on Enneagram is *The Pathway Back to You* by Ian Cronn). The numbers on the Enneagram represent nine different strategies of relating to ourselves. It's based on the survival skills that we picked up as kids. At the time, they served us well. They were part of how we learned to cope with being typical human children in typical human families. But when we carry them into adulthood, they stop serving us. The original reasons we picked them up are gone, and where they once provided us with comfort and growth, they now actually (mostly) hinder our relationships and growth.

The gift of the Enneagram is that it shows us how those skills we learned can be used as strengths and also how we fall into them as weaknesses. I learned that I'm a Peacemaker. One of the attributes of a peacemaker is wanting to maintain peace in relationships, and wanting to be liked. I actually hated this and resisted it when I read it. How selfish! How self-centered! How... not Godly. I didn't want to want to be liked. I wanted to think I didn't care and had thick skin. But, I don't. And I want to be liked. And I brought this into my parenting.

Why do I want to be liked?

Because I've made up a story that being liked means I'm worthy of love and belonging. If I'm not liked, the story tells me that I'm not worthy of love and belonging. That I'm an unwanted mistake. That I'm unnecessary on this planet. You can imagine as a hormonal teen how heavy this was to believe. Leaving my worth and value in the hands of angsty, insecure, under-developed teenage peers was not the highlight of my life. I was in deep, deep pain and struggled with wanting to live. Teenage years bled into college years bled into married years and into parenting. And while I found much healing, an identity in the family of God, and friends to help me confront the story, it still lingered as a strong thread in my quiet motivation. It wasn't until years into parenting children of trauma that I realized what the huge rub was for me. I was looking for my kids to prove to me that I was lovable and worthy of belonging. Surely, all of my goodness and kindness and helpfulness would make them like me, thus making me believe I was worthy.

Yep, we come to our parenting with our own invisible luggage. Mine was packed full.

Really, this means I played into the hands of my kids' manipulation. They could sniff weakness like this miles away and capitalize on it for their own survival. They learned how to keep me in the cycle of being my very best for them *all the time* while withholding the affirmation I longed for—just out of reach. Crazy, right? I had no idea I was even caught in this cycle. Until one day I began to see it. I began to see how twisted it was that I was waiting for my kids to prove me worthy of my own life. I share this in full vulnerability. Maybe you're not as twisted and broken as I am, but I know we all bring our stuff, and it gets mixed right in with their stuff. And we look like the hot mess that we feel.

Fortunately, I believe God brought this to my awareness, both for my healing and for theirs. Because I couldn't be a truly good mom, the thing I most desired, until I'd addressed this brokenness in myself. I needed to do the work of nailing down who I am and why I'm worthy of love and belonging just by being me before I could help my kids find it for themselves. It's a journey I'm still on in all the other areas of my life, but one I'm grateful I can now see. This search for worth has trapped me in fear and caused me to miss amazing life opportunities. Recognizing my worth has likewise opened incredible doors for impact and influence as I share my stories of Hard to Healing, opportunities I missed while hiding in my corner of shame.

When I was stuck in the cycle, I was also the Nurturing Enemy for my kids. In order to survive, they had to find reasons not to like me. Liking me was terrifying. It meant I could hurt and disappoint them, just as their first mother had done. My issues triggered their issues! Add to the mix an unsuspecting partner (who also brings their stuff to the parenting role). They see a divide between the child and their targeted parent, but they often don't understand the divide.

My husband didn't. He felt caught in the middle between a grown woman who needed to pull her pants up (being the bigger person) and a child who, yeah, was irritating but was just a kid. As I talked about in Chapter 9, he felt stuck. It took our marriage coming to a very rocky place before we could address the dynamics at work here. And it took that article from the Institute for Attachment to help us recognize, validate, and move beyond the crazy cycle we were stuck in. (We will talk about the further impact on marriage in the next chapter).

If you're connecting with this dance, hopefully, you now understand why you seem to have it harder than your partner. Hopefully, it speaks to your doubts about whether it's just you, why you can't seem to be the "better" person, and why it's so hard. Or, if you've found yourself feeling in the middle of your child and your spouse, hopefully, you recognize now that there's a dynamic going on, and you might be in the way. Make sure to read the next chapter on marital impact for some guidance on how to stop the triangulation dance with your kids.

REPUTATION

For our purposes, reputation falls under two types: public and internal. Our sense of integrity is based on our internal reputation. For example, if I began to foster children so I could help kids, to save them from certain destruction, and then I fail, my internal reputation is corrupted. I didn't live up to my own value. This brings about feelings of shame. It brings up doubts about our own trustworthiness and abilities. It's humbling and embarrassing to realize we can't live up to our own ideals. And since we avoid shame and embarrassment, we work hard to prevent this kind of failure. This means we deal with unlimited levels of stress and anxiety, putting pressures on ourselves and our kids to resolve our deficiencies. This brings us back to being self-aware of our own childhood traumas, our own survival skills, and the luggage we bring to this relationship.

We are also confronted by our public reputation. Having CPS come to our home is scary for a variety of reasons, but our reputation falls into this as well. I've known people to respond very defensively when the conversation of CPS-to-their-home visits come up. We don't want to be seen as people who abuse children, and we all associate CPS with abusive parenting. Or abusive-looking enough that the government had to come check in. That someone suspected abuse and called them to check it out. We don't want to be seen as one of these families. Unfortunately, our children and their need for attention often brings CPS to our homes. And while they leave, dismissing our cases, it's still fear-inducing, stress-raising, and threatening to our reputations.

Even if CPS doesn't come out to our homes, we have the judgments and misplaced perspectives of our friends and family to address. Their questions and judgments challenge our desire to be reputable people. Our children and their behaviors at school give us a reputation in the classroom and at school events. Often our children aren't invited to birthday parties because they're "that" kid. So we become "that" family. This feeds back into the isolation we experience. The impact of raising these children isn't limited to our own personal doubts and fears, or the luggage we bring to the relationship, but can actually alter or cost us our public reputation. We will work hard to protect our image internally and publicly, but doing it while raising our children with AD is a losing battle.

Or at least it seems so.

One of the things we've learned is to continue being who we are. To not always rise in defense of ourselves, but to let our love and lives speak for themselves. There were times I wanted to grab a megaphone and stand in a very public place. "Dear city, if you have had any conversations about us with any of our children, please see me to get both sides." This desire made me aware of how much I was being affected by knowing there were conversations happening that I couldn't control. But what I *could* control is who I am and how I live my life.

For the people who wanted to know the full story, I could trust that they'd come to us directly with concerns. And I could trust that anyone lacking that maturity would come to their own conclusions. But this was their responsibility, not mine. I could put a healthy boundary around what I would be responsible for. There were some who came to us, willing to hear our story, to learn and grow and walk with us. And there were some who didn't. Some persisted in believing our kids with AD and didn't have the maturity or life experience or courage to come to the parents and talk through the stories they'd heard. And that's okay. I've learned by now that those people end up gaining the life experience they need (often by ending up in my shoes one way or another). And who knows, maybe they come around. And maybe they don't.

As we do our own work to refuse shame and false stories in our own identity, we are less fazed by these people and their own journey toward maturity. And as we live the integrity of our lives, we prove ourselves, and our kids prove themselves, and people calm down. After we'd been in any community for awhile, our children's lies seemed much less likely to the people around us. They'd been in our home, gotten to know us, know our kids, and knew when a healthy-looking child said they weren't being fed that they actually were and that we had taken in children with unique needs.

Our lives, lived with integrity, became our best defense. As far as living with our internal reputation, well that was addressed as well. As soon as we could accept what wasn't in our control and own what was, we found a lot more grace for ourselves. And as we did the hard work of revisiting our earlier motivations for fostering and adopting, we could reframe and restructure our belief systems. Rather than "saving" kids as we'd originally dreamed, we were equipping kids. Or giving them ten more years of life off the streets, off drugs, and not pregnant. Once we recognized some of our earlier faulty thinking and adjusted it to reality, we found our inner reputation intact. We also learned that humility, apology, and forgiveness for ourselves and others go a long way.

Now that we've covered the impact of raising children with AD on us personally, let's look at the impact on our marriages and then on our birth children. Let's continue to move forward with hope into a future of healing with these kiddos!

CHAPTER 15

IMPACT ON MARRIAGE

O ne of the other things I didn't expect in raising foster and adopted children was the impact it would have on my marriage.

We are a little backward from many families we've met.

The first three years of our marriage could be summed up by "two mighty rivers converging into one." We knew there would be smoother waters ahead, but man, getting there was rapid-riding bumpy! There were certainly other major factors that enhanced those rapids (one of those "factors" can be found in our book, *While We Slept: Finding Hope and Healing After Homicide*), but even without those, we were painfully learning how to make our two lives one.

When we had kids, we found our calmer waters. Where we'd only had each other to worry about before, we now found a united front in raising up kids. We agreed in many ways on how to parent. We teamed up and found unity. Not that everything leading up was conflict. We'd made some good progress. But having children was catalytic for us finding harmony as a couple. This is what was backward. Most families we talk to did great *until* they had kids. However you arrived at the moment of parenting, there were likely challenges. This is as true with your birth children, as it is with adopted children, as it is with adopted children with AD.

Given how much parenting had bonded us, we were completely blind-sided by how it could also tear us apart. After seven years of parenting them, I found myself completely depleted by our children with AD. We didn't have a solid diagnosis for them at the time, but we knew it was hard work. And even in the hard, we were such a great team. On days when I was just *done*, my husband usually had what we needed to step up and dig into the hard. I'd pass the baton and he'd run. I'd regroup and position myself on the line. He'd come running around the corner, about to pass out, handing the baton back to me. Round and round we went.

Until I began needing him to take the baton more often. Drained. Beat down. Confused. Dealing with my own inadequacy, my own shame at failing at this parenting thing, and trying to understand why in the world these kids were so hard. It wasn't until I learned about the Nurturing Enemy that it all fell into place.

Folks, our kids are smart kids. They're strategic. My husband wasn't dealing with the daily phone calls and emails and conversations that I was. The lies weren't always about him specifically as they were about me. The kids were still hard for him, but he definitely saw more of the sweet and charming sides. He'd have a talk with them about their behavior and they'd cry and share how hard they try to love me. Oh, man. He would mediate conversations using our skills from marriage classes. They'd confide their "secrets" and pain with him, a sacred space and they knew it. He felt like he was making progress. (They're so good at making people, even therapists, feel like they're making progress. Meanwhile, they're feeding you just enough to satiate you while staying at a safe distance).

It was at my lowest, one of our child's lowest, coupled with my husband's cluelessness that led us to a serious marital counseling session. My own pain was so intense that I could hardly see a way out. I had read an article on how many men end up divorced from marriages where they hadn't even known there was a problem. I was drowning fast and needed his support. He was stuck between me and our child. We got help!

In Chapter 9, I shared how we all processed this Triangulation Dance. My husband had to choose to stand with his partner and stop trying to bridge our child and me. Instead of trying to help our child understand me, and me understand our child, he began to support me through dialogue, empathy, and attention. My husband also put an end to conversations that were about *me* but with *him*.

These small shifts in our home were major for our health. It was also important for my husband to recognize *his* luggage. He found he also had a need for approval and was satisfying it in the seemingly open conversations he had with our children with AD. He realized approval from our children was fickle, but his connection to me as his wife was sane and lasting. We continued forward with the aid of our therapist and our commitment to regaining our footing with each other. Our children quickly realized they couldn't beat down this new united front.

When I asked my husband to reflect on his experience from those years, he remembers that this was largely tied to his hope that our teen was "normal." He wanted to give our child all of the freedoms of a typical adolescent. We were surrounded by families of typical adolescents. Friends were saying to him, "He's just a normal kid; seems like your wife is being too hard on him." Feedback from people *not* living in our home about kids they thought were "normal." And he recognized his people-pleasing nature. Pleasing our children would mean being liked and being on their good side with all the rewards. (Our own abandonment stuff is real.)

As soon as he stepped out from the middle, trusted that our child was not typical and needed unique parameters to address his different wiring, he began to see it. My husband had to step out of his people-pleasing, gain objectivity, and take a different path to the healthy relationships we all wanted.

At a recent speaking engagement, my husband also addressed the ways he'd checked out. He had engaged in a full load of numbing behaviors, leaving the wreckage to a drowning wife. He couldn't fix what was happening, and rather than braving the rough waters and possibly failing, he left. Not physically, but emotionally. He spent hours in front of a screen to turn off the pain of our household. This only further tore at the connection we so desperately needed to do this job well. I felt the overwhelming load of being left to do everything alone while he went to work, hid behind a screen, or people-pleased our children. One day, he says, he "woke up" and realized that he'd missed a chunk of life. Suddenly he was filled with conviction to take the reins in our crumbling home and effect positive change.

As soon as my husband began redirecting our child toward healthy conflict management and joined me in appropriately restricting freedoms, our child changed strategies. Coincidentally, he also began to fail in bigger ways with the freedoms he'd already been given by my husband. Previously, my husband would hand out a freedom, I'd predict what was going to happen if it was given, and I'd nail it. My husband began to recognize the patterns I'd been addressing. When he stopped defending the freedoms and began implementing healthy parameters, our child began slandering his dad where it had been almost uniquely about me. Our child began to find new community members who would "stand up to us" so he could have what he wanted. (We did at one time try to hand over all of the desired freedoms, just to see how it would go. It went bad. But we tried that too!). My husband quickly realized that where he'd thought he'd had a good relationship with his child, he'd actually been a tool in our child's hands. He was being used. All of the evidence pointed to triangulation.

I shared this chapter with another adoptive dad. He said, "That's exactly what happened with us, too." He went on to share how he'd believed his wife was being too strict, that the teen was challenging, sure, but with more love from mom, she could be fine. But when he began supporting his wife, the tables turned and he saw the worst of what that kid could offer—a "gift" he'd had the blessing of missing out on while he was buddy-buddy.

Until this moment of recognition, our marriage while parenting our children was one of suspicion, judgment, accusation, good guy/bad guy, the middle man, and a lot of confusion. We loved each other. We knew we had the same goals in parenting. We knew we loved our kids. But we couldn't figure out why it was so hard for me. Or why I was so exhausted. Or why I was the bad parent. I mean, who doesn't want to be the *good* parent? But for some reason, I just wasn't enough. Or so we thought.

Taking the time to get some professional help gave us guidance and objectivity. It gave us a new perspective. It gave us pause to stop and reflect on what mattered to us, where we were falling short, and a mediator of sorts to help us move beyond the struggles. Mind you, I started this chapter with two converging rivers. Clearly, we didn't need the help of a child to have struggles. However, getting caught up in the triangulation, manipulation, and charm of our child with AD only served to shake up and deteriorate what we had built.

I'd love to see a statistic of divorce among families raising children with AD. I know many families personally who have lived on the brink. While I don't know the numbers (and can't find that anyone has researched it), I know people personally who've divorced or contemplated it. This business of raising exhausting kids is enough to deteriorate any partnership.

If this is you, and you're married and co-parenting a child with AD, start with a conversation. Take a date, a break, a visit to a therapist, and start talking. The Nurturing Enemy is often feeling isolated, guilty, responsible, inadequate, ashamed, embarrassed, confused, angry, exhausted, and sad. Lots of sad. They may not know how to put words to all the crazy they feel. Listen well to one another, without judgment or accusation. Respond with active listening and empathy. Be a safe place for the other to share their own sense of insufficiency and sadness, their fear that they aren't enough to help this kid. Be willing to commit to being each other's biggest support. Revive compassion and believe the best in the other person. Your partner may not see the child's behavior the same way (nor experience the brunt of it) as the Nurturing Enemy does. Likewise, the "good cop" needs to share their experience. Are they feeling stuck in the middle? Responsible to mediate? Enjoying what feels like a growing relationship with this child finally? What would it look like to support your spouse? To stand with him or her? To refuse to be in the middle? Communicate.

If you feel concerned that you can't listen well because of your own hurt and frustration, bring a trusted friend or counselor into the conversation to get you going. This is the second biggest decision we made that saved our marriage. Our first biggest decision was on our wedding day, when we committed before *God* to love and honor our spouse, no matter what. Well, we were living the no-matter-what and we needed support to honor our commitment. Finding it saved us.

A healthy, intact, growing marriage is more effective in raising kids with AD. Try as they might to separate us, they need to experience that they *can't*. This builds a foundation of safety. If they can wreck us, then they have the power, which keeps them stuck! Prioritize taking care of your marriage as a *huge* step in loving them.

Alright! Let's take a look at the impact of raising children with AD on birth children.

CHAPTER 16

IMPACT ON BIRTH CHILDREN

*Note: I chose to use the phrase "birth children" in this chapter because they make up the majority of the population I refer to. It is meant to indicate any child living in the home who does not have an attachment disorder such as a step child, a grandchild, or even an adopted child! When reading, insert your particular AD-free child as appropriate.

One of the scariest things for us was what the impact of raising children of trauma alongside birth children would be. When we began certification for foster care, I was on a seven-year plan for birthing a child. Meaning, I wanted seven years of marriage before we tried. (I have no idea why seven.) As we began investigating foster care, we attended a Christmas dinner with a foster agency. During that meal, a teenager shared her experience as a birth daughter being raised alongside adopted children. She shared how each child who'd passed through had become a sister or a brother. She talked about sharing her room. Growing in compassion. She was inspirational. She was key to our decision to go ahead and start certifying. My husband, especially, wasn't on board as quickly as I was. He wanted to get to know other families, ask questions, and especially hear from biological children. This Christmas dinner won him over and we started the process.

We began certifying for foster care in year two of our marriage. When we certified, our foster family agency said we could certify fost-adopt, just in case we decided to adopt a child. Ya know, in case. We said sure.

Well, wouldn't you know it, but toward the end of our certification process, I got pregnant. We finished certifying but put everything on hold to give us time to have a baby. When our firstborn was three months old, even though we had a pause on our foster placement plan, we got a phone call. Two children needed respite. One of the children had a known sexual abuse history, and the other didn't. We opted for the one who didn't. So in moved an eight-year-old boy for the weekend. And by now you know our story.

Over a decade later, we have raised two birth children alongside two adopted children alongside multiple foster children and various other housemates (including Syrian refugees, military children, A Peruvian homeless woman, etc.). Not only this, but we've walked with many families who've done the same. And we've seen the patterns time and again.

Our birth children are heavily impacted by our decision to join them with foster and adopted children.

In fact, some studies have come to call our birth children the Voiceless Population.[1] Decisions are made to join them with brand new siblings, often without asking them, and many times without preparing them. At whatever age new siblings join the family, birth children become aware of trauma and loss far earlier than they should. This was certainly true for our children. Not only did they have to come to understand why and how a parent couldn't care for their own child, but they also had to live alongside the manifestation of trauma that our foster/adopted kids exposed them too. This was apparent to me in playdates with children not being raised alongside children with AD who were still naive and innocent to some of the harsh realities my kids were aware of.

Our birth children are voiceless because they are not given an opportunity to talk about how they feel about the changes. And if they do, consider this: If you've communicated that the right and loving thing to do is welcome strangers into your home and raise them with love, is their space for a birth child to say, "No, I don't like this."? It puts them in conflict with the family and its values. Some birth children have expressed feeling a great amount of regret and shame anytime they held a negative feeling about the additions to their family. This was good and right, wasn't it? So how could they think something negative? At such a young age, our children don't want to disappoint or be in conflict with us. Even if asked, they may feel unable to share their true feelings of guilt and fear.

So our birth children are thrown into a new family situation. What was familiar, changes for them. Or if they were birthed into the situation, as our youngest was, they don't ever have an opportunity to voice their thoughts—it just is.

And so begins the first steps of a lifetime of impact by their parents' decision. They experience abandonment, sacrifice, loss, trauma, unrealistic expectations, fear, abuse, anxiety, confusion, and resentment to name a few. Are there positive impacts on our children? Yes, there are! (I'll talk about some in a minute.) But they are often overshadowed by the challenges that force them quietly into a corner.

When we move children with higher needs into our home, which any adopted child has, but especially children with AD, we immediately welcome a child who will need more of our time, attention, and energy. This naturally moves our relatively need-free birth children to the backseat of the family. As the needs of the adopted child grow, and as more adopted children join, the more the "bad kids" tend to suck the energy, leaving the "good kids" with what's left. Parents are frazzled trying to cope with AD behaviors and end up depleted emotionally and physically.

My heart breaks to think of how often this happened in our home. We tried to be aware of it, and still, we'd get sucked back into the vortex of AD over and over. A three-hour conversation of crazy with a kid, while my birth child entertained themselves, trying to stay out of the way and not need anything. Or the entire year when I crashed. Or as my counselor said, I expired. All of my survival skills gave up on me and I slept for about a year. I'd wake up to go pick up my daughter from kindergarten at noon. She would sit on the bed next to me and play an educational game, watch a Netflix show, or read books, and I'd sleep again until dinner. I wanted so badly to be awake with her, to play games, to give her my undivided attention. This was our year! She was the baby, and it was just *us* while everyone was still at school. Such a rare time between a baby in the family and her parent. And I slept through a whole year of it.

Finally, in desperation, I went to the doctor to have my thyroid checked again. This is the time we showed up, my daughter in rain boots and a princess dress, and her mama a hot mess. I cried to the doctor about my fatigue and how I needed the energy for my children with AD when they get home from school. Note, I wasn't crying because I couldn't stay awake for my daughter (though that was truly a deep grief). Instead, I was crying because I wanted enough emotional and physical energy to cope with the never ending challenges of my children with AD.

She helped me "bridge" this time in my life, and it was exactly what I needed. I slowly came out of my slumber and was present with my daughter. We had picnics in the yard, playdates, games, dates. But still, I missed a whole year. My husband and I began to realize how much we were being pulled from our other kiddos. How hard they worked to be perfect so as not to bring any more hardship to their parents.

One of my children has dealt with extreme perfectionism his whole life (and his whole life has been alongside children with AD). He is very hard on himself. We have to remind him all the time that mistakes are our greatest teacher and our home is a safe place to make them. But one day he said, "Mom, what if I'm hard like the other kids when I grow up, too? What if I do the same things they do?" He was only seven or eight, and he was afraid he'd be hard on us. Afraid that he'd do *anything* that would cause us more pain than what he'd already watched us survive. We've had lots of talks and try to demonstrate with every opportunity that we work through hard things together, as a family. That our home is safe, and we are safe. That he can be free to be himself. We even point out how we love our other kids deeply, even if that love looks different from some families. But so many years of experiencing our pain has had its consequences. It's a battle we continue to fight and we're not giving up. But the impact is real.

Our birth kids are expected to cope with problematic situations in our home. Yet they are children! They've had no training. Shoot, *we've* had no training! They are told to provide love and patience, to share their things, their parents, their lives. Yet they are underserved, under-seen, and missed.

The System gives resources to the family for the foster children: money, healthcare, therapy, new clothes, an allowance... but birth children don't get anything. And if the family can't afford it, birth children don't get the therapy they need, and the impact on them can be huge! I remember the foster agency bringing gifts to our foster kids each year. Donations made to them. Provisions made for them. We had to buy them fifty dollars worth of brand new clothes every month, even though we shopped second-hand. Birth children are often neglected in these gifts. And not only in the gifts, but in the actual services as well. While we were raising our kids, I didn't know of one single service made available to my birth children for navigating this decision we'd made for them. Now that half our kids are launched, I've learned of one single support group for birth children ages eleven to fifteen. I'm so grateful for it, yet it still neglects my nine-year-old daughter. The services are insufficient for these invisible children.

I would love a place for my kids to process their anxiety. To this day, if I am stressed about anything, my kids feel it and visibly respond. One of my children takes on the role of peacemaker. She wants harmony and unity. She'll want to comfort me, be physically close and connected, and ask how I'm doing. She's nine. In a family therapy session, she shared that she feels like the protector in our family. It's her job to help everyone feel better. That's a huge task for a child, and I know many birth children take this on.

My son, on the other hand, becomes very serious, focused, and limited in his ability to cope with his own mistakes in response to our stress. In his effort to not add to our pain, he refuses to be human.

Some kids feel anxiety about sharing their resources, whether they're emotional or material. They've sacrificed their parents for the good of these new siblings, only to find that the siblings aren't grateful for the parents they were given. Some birth children end up feeling resentful at the fact that their sacrifice was for naught. For the sake of the family value or vision, they made way for these kids to take the best of Mom and Dad, only to have these siblings slander, tear down, yell at, threaten, and harm their parents.

One of the children we raised spent three hours telling our birth children what awful people we are. When we came into the situation, unknowingly, our younger children hid, telling us what happened from their hiding places. They were afraid of what would be done to them for telling us! We had no idea this was happening and I'm so glad they were brave to tell us. But it didn't change that they experienced it.

This leads to so much confusion. Sometimes our kids with AD are good siblings but awful sons and daughters. Sometimes our birth children are resented by the adopted children with AD because they get a good childhood with loving parents. And in their own pain, feel envy and anger toward the birth children. We witnessed many relationships between birth and adopted siblings that broke down because of this. Even though the adopted children were given the best of the parents, they missed it. And they missed it by being angry at the birth children for getting to stay with their birth families. Not having a clue how much their behavior was robbing those same children of experiencing the best of their birth parents.

And finally, our kids sometimes suffer actual, physical harm. There are heartbreaking stories of molestation, physical abuse, and emotional abuse. Our children experienced some of those things. When one of our birth children was very young, the boundarylessness of one of our children with AD began to take a toll. Our child couldn't hear "no" nor could this child read social cues. Our toddler would say "No" and try to have some personal space, but the older sibling wouldn't give it. I remember a day when the toddler was on the couch and this older sibling approached the far end of it—and touched the couch. The toddler had a meltdown. He was so used to having his personal space violated that his bubble became as large as the couch. This led to over a decade of our vigilance in protecting boundaries, aiding said child in respecting the "no" of another, on and on.

Our birth children have a ton to deal with. And I imagine a chapter like this makes a family want to quit adoption right now. But I love what a grown birth child, Eshele Williams, PsyD LMFT, said of her experience raised with adopted children. She said,

I was impacted, but I am not broken.[2]

Amen! She talks about the strength she has because of her journey searching for and finding her voice. She's an advocate for birth children and adoptive families, and she's bringing awareness to our homes.

Our birth children are impacted, but not broken.

They really do learn compassion, grow in empathy, are slow to judge other families, and develop perseverance, character, hope, and humility. Learning to cope at such young ages has given them skills. They've learned how to love challenging people. They've learned to see *beyond* the challenges, to the person of deep value beneath. After everything my birth children have witnessed and experienced, my daughter said, "I miss my older siblings!" (who've grown up and moved out). It's confusing and complicated. But at the end of the day, they are brother and sister. Not "adopted" brother and sister. Not "broken" brother and sister. Not "the others." They are just brother and sister, and they are loved and missed. Our kids know how to love the hard-to-love. They know about boundaries, about faithfulness, about resilience. Our birth children are resilient.

And today is the day to give them a voice.

Ask them about their process. Include them in decision-making. Spend intentional time with them. Don't save the last and least for them.

One day recently, my youngest daughter said to me, "Mom, you really are a wonder mom." I paused and looked up at her. I asked her to elaborate, curious about what had brought on such sweet, unprompted words. "You give up your sleep for me when I'm sick, and you take care of me. I love the job you have (coaching and writing) because you help people, and I love that when your job is done, you spend time with me." Naturally, this brought tears to my eyes. What a gift. It also prompted me to apologize, again, for the year she sat beside me sleeping, reading, or watching a show. It's a guilt I need to hand over and free myself of. "But Mom, that's how [my brother] and I got close. When he came home from school, we played and played. That's why we are best friends."

She gave me a gift, a glimpse into her experience being "set aside" while kids with greater needs got the best of my limited energy. While I wear it in shame, she wears it as the reason she and her brother are best buds. And they are! Tears fill my eyes as I write this.

Yes, they played and played. They played for the hours-long conversations between their older siblings and us. They played when big-kid-sized tantrums were thrown. They played when we lost our cool. They paused when we apologized and tried to regroup. And then they played some more. A bond formed between them that was fashioned from hardship, which now bears the marks beautifully.

As we came to understand AD and its impact on our birth kids, we began to set timers for the minutes we'd allocate to dealing with one of our children with AD. When that timer went off, done. We left the interaction wherever it was, and intentionally found a child who would most likely fall through the cracks and spent purposeful time with them. We established dates with our birth children. We took them on one-on-one personal retreats with us. Sometimes our kids with AD missed out on an event as a consequence, but we still took the other children. No more missing out on fun things just because the child with AD couldn't handle it. Whenever we felt ourselves getting sucked into the vortex of AD manipulation and magnetism, we'd step back and say, "Nope! Not today. Not anymore." We established boundaries in our home that invited any child who wanted to relate in a healthy manner to the game, event, or dinner. And whoever couldn't, could sit it out.

We redirected our attention, time, and energy. We also had to be super intentional with our own self-care. We started marital and individual therapy, connecting with accountability partners, monitoring our bedtimes, joining support groups, participating in creative activities, guarding our conversations around the younger children, praying together, playing together, and trying to keep the attention on the kids who were seeking it appropriately. And in many ways, it worked. Our older kids couldn't yank on us and get the previous response. We offered them positive attention wherever we could. We also took them on one-on-ones and reached out. But we also didn't get sucked into the chase.

Find ways to dedicate time and attention to each kid, yes, but especially to the ones in your home who are trying to stay under the radar. The ones who are sacrificing their parents for these other children. Who weren't asked if they'd like to share their home and parents with strangers. To the kids trying to keep it together so they don't add another smidge of pain to your life.

And show yourself grace. I could grieve over my missed years with them then, or miss moments now. And I should grieve. But if I stay there, I miss the moments I have now. We've talked with our kids, asked their forgiveness, and began a new journey of healing together. Find ways to do the same, regardless of how old they are.

We've covered some hard things. The impact on our families, ourselves, and our kids with AD is *big*. It's real. *But it's not hopeless.* And you are not alone. Let's move into Section 3, where we will take a look at treatment options families have tried. I'll be upfront—there's a lot to be done in the way of effective treatment for our kids, but there are ways to make progress. Let's start there.

SECTION 3

A person who never learned to TRUST confuses intensity with closeness, obsession with care, and control with security.

—*Patrick Carnes, psychiatrist*

CHAPTER 17

CURRENT TREATMENT OPTIONS

One of the most disheartening realities around attachment disorders is our options for treatment.

Yet, here is a chapter with my attempt at both giving some guidance and reassurance.

First, the reassurance.

This is too much for your family to handle alone.

This *is* reassuring. And if you're a parent or family member who has given everything to see this kid healed and have had little to show for it, this is why: You can not bring complete healing to this child. That is why attempt after attempt has led to so little permanent change. It can't be enough. It's not because you aren't a good parent or even a loving parent. It's not because you weren't cut out for this and should never have had children, however they came to you. It's not because you're broken or just can't pull up your bootstraps and be the adult. It's not because you're a bad, neglectful parent. It's not because you're crazy. It's not for any of the reasons that have crossed your mind, plagued your thoughts, or been tossed at you by outsiders looking in.

It's because your child has a traumatized brain. And that traumatized brain is still being studied and understood. And basically, we're just in the beginning stages of realizing the effect of trauma on people, let alone little children pre-birth. The conversation is still relatively new, but growing louder daily. Finally we have people talking about the trauma we experience as parents or how to actually bring health and healing to our kids and to ourselves. But there's still a lot we don't know.

To date, there isn't a medication or guaranteed treatment for curing these disorders. There are medications that are used to treat some of the symptoms, like anxiety or hyperactivity. There are medications to treat some of the other disorders that often show up in conjunction, like ADHD or depression, which our kids are more likely to have. But an attachment disorder on its own really doesn't yet have any effective medicinal treatment. Nothing has worked for a significant number of people consistently.

What does this mean for you? That you can do your very best, and you will still fall short. Because everything, so far, has fallen short.

But.

That doesn't mean all of the trying is wasted or that it doesn't help at least a little in getting through today. It does mean that you need to work on your expectations for possible outcomes. Know that you might spend money, and nothing will change. Know that you might decide not to spend the money and then wonder endlessly if you should have and whether or not it would have worked. Be aware of your own motivations and needs, your own capacity and boundaries, and make decisions for your child's best from there.

The following is a look at some of the treatments that families like ours are trying, have tried, hope to try. For some families, a relative degree of success has occurred, but not for all. The honest answer is there hasn't been the one solid thing that "fixes" our kids. What has helped has been extremely expensive and had short-term success. There are some strategies we picked up from articles that worked in our house and might work in yours. And by "work" I mean, gave us what we needed to get our kids to adulthood. I'll share those in the next chapter. But first, let's talk about the out-of-home possibilities of care for our kiddos.

INPATIENT CARE

There are a variety of Residential Treatment Centers (RTC) where a child with AD can go live temporarily with therapeutic parents trained in bonding and healing work. These run from $7000-$24,000+ per month. These have seemed to be effective in two ways. One, the family gets a much-needed break. There is time to work on some self- and family-healing. To pause from the chaos that is home. And do some good healing work interpersonally and with the child while they are at a distance. Most of these homes require regular visits and calls to work on healthy family reunification. You get to work on healing with your kid while having actual physical distance between you to heal. Secondly, these help the child very specifically. The goal is to help them learn how to attach in healthy ways, to process the trauma in their amygdala, and return to healthier functioning.

I've seen children come back from programs like this and, for a time, do relatively well. I haven't seen very many situations (if any) where the "healing" was permanent. At some point, the children return to their former behaviors. Whether this is a failure of the treatment, the environment they return to (our homes, where we are their trigger and our habits are in place), or a combination, we're not sure. And not all RTCs are created equal. Some seem to totally get attachment disorders and have specially trained staff. Others seem to be more generalized for "hard" kids and can actually cause more harm than help, providing ineffective strategies and being triangulated at the same time. If you go this route, be sure to do a lot of research, including interviewing other families. When we searched for a treatment center, we asked inside the RAD support groups on Facebook, we asked our Adoption Assistance Program, and the therapist who was currently working with our children. After a lot of searching and inquiry, we found a place that seemed great in Tahoe for $7,000/month. But just as we were about to put our kid on a plane, the facility realized our child would soon turn eighteen years old and his government funding for the program would be cut to $1400/month. They retracted their acceptance.

SPECIALIZED ATTACHMENT-BASED THERAPY

The term "Attachment Therapy" comes with a lot of baggage, so be aware of this as you begin your own research. Attachment therapy (as opposed to attachment-based therapy) has a history of treatments called "holding" and "rebirthing." To my knowledge, Colorado has banned "rebirthing" because of a death that occurred during this treatment. I've known a few families personally who used Attachment therapy and found it helpful for their children and their homes. And I know others who are very leery of it. Attachment therapy is pretty controversial, so do your due diligence in research before choosing (or not choosing) that path.

Attachment-based therapy, on the other hand, is more like traditional therapy but, for our kids, far more effective. Attachment-based therapists are studied and skilled in navigating the unique challenges our families face, the causes of trauma and attachment dysfunction in our kids, and are considerably less likely to be manipulated into a triangulating relationship. Some of the children I parented had years of traditional therapy, which sometimes caused more harm than not. However, when we finally accessed Attachment-based therapy, we were relieved when, after a few months, the therapist hadn't turned against us or our parenting. It was the first time we actually felt safe, heard, and helped, and we all walked toward healing together. Unfortunately, our children made decisions to leave therapy after only a few months and we didn't see enough change to personally experience the effectiveness of it. The therapist did tell us that it takes *years* of therapy for a child or adult with AD to begin forming healthy relationships.

The goal of Attachment-based therapy is to help the family heal. It's to help the child overcome their "stuckness" and work toward forming healthy relationships. And it's to help the parents heal from their own attachment insecurities to best serve and truly love their child in the best possible way. For us, it's about rebuilding our own resiliency and capacity so that we can keep at it. And for them, it's to help them begin to experience love as it was designed to be experienced. The focus is really on emotional healing for all.

Eye Movement Desensitization and Reprocessing (EMDR)

I love how EMDR therapist, Dr. Arielle Schwartz explains EMDR in the article, *Healing Attachment Trauma with EMDR Therapy*:

> We now realize that the brain may be 're-wired' by relationships throughout our lifespan. Healthy relationships allow us to shape and be shaped in the directions that most serve us. The challenge is that we tend to re-create relationships that match what we know. Deep inside we may expect to be rejected and we enact this expectation by either choosing a partner who is rejecting or acting in a manner which evokes that response in another. Psychotherapy helps clients take responsibility for their part of perpetuating this dynamic. [1]

This brain-based therapy has shown effectiveness in reducing the symptoms of PTSD, and I believe this is its most common use. However, a number of families have experienced help for their child and themselves with EMDR. It uses knowledge of how the brain works to strategically "trick" your brain into recategorizing (and thus pushing traumatic events out of the amygdala) so you can truly heal, from the brain out. It's important that the EMDR therapist has experience with attachment specifically. Even in EMDR, a therapist who is unfamiliar with attachment dysfunction can be ineffective. They must understand the nuances of attachment distortion to strategize treatment for the best outcome. So be sure to ask about this.

Brain Spotting (BSP)

Brain Spotting is an offshoot of EMDR, though similar in purpose. The major difference appears to be that BSP is less over-stimulating and therefore more people can participate. Another difference is that EMDR uses a strict protocol and multiple eye movements (used to access various parts of the brain. Crazy, I know!). BSP, on the other hand, has a lot of freedom for therapists to cater their technique to their specific client. It also focuses on a single position of the eye versus rapid movements. An article on *Good Therapy* explains it this way,

> According to therapist and creator David Grand, the direction in which people look or gaze can affect the way they feel. During brainspotting, therapists help people position their eyes in ways that enable them to target sources of negative emotion. With the aid of a pointer, trained brainspotting therapists slowly guide the eyes of people in therapy across their field of vision to find appropriate 'brainspots,' with a brainspot being an eye position that activates a traumatic memory or painful emotion. Practitioners of the procedure believe it allows therapists to access emotions on a deeper level and target the physical effects of trauma.[2]

While this was originally developed to help individuals with PTSD, the practice seems to be showing its effectiveness in helping people with unprocessed trauma find healing as well.

BRAINPAINT

I have the privilege of knowing the lead BrainPaint practitioner in my area, which led to a personal conversation between the founder and I. I find BrainPaint fascinating, and am learning more about it with these critical relationships. I have many friends using BrainPaint for healing among adults and children alike. It's a neurotherapy that uses computer programming to communicate with your brain! Straight from the BrainPaint website,

Just as your brain makes sense of information being fed to it from gravity, it makes sense of the information being conveyed to it by the software. The brain is an organ that processes substantially more information than your mind could handle. Your mind can not even see, hear, smell, taste or consciously feel earth's gravitational pull, yet your brain is constantly sending neural commands to muscles according to feedback it receives from gravity. Even though your mind wants to understand and even participate in your neurofeedback session, it is your brain that we are training.[3]

Clients begin with an assessment. Then a treatment plan is formed. When the treatment phase begins, sensors are placed on the client's scalp to pick up on electrical activity coming from the brain. It feeds this information to the computer program which looks for areas that aren't working as efficiently.

EEG biofeedback, via software, gives the brain a way to see itself in action. The brain then learns how to better self-regulate its states of thoughts, feelings and arousal levels. EEG biofeedback works as if the computer screen is a mirror for the brain; it magnifies areas that are not working as efficiently as they could, and trains the brain to operate more effectively. The brain then reorganizes itself by forming new neural pathways or activating unused ones as it expands functionality. As with all abilities we develop, the gains made with EEG biofeedback are typically permanent.

BrainPaint has proven to be successful with many behaviors, such as those connected to ADHD, anxiety, depression, PTSD, trauma, addiction, physical pain, and more. Many of my friends with children with AD are looking at BrainPaint as an option and finding levels of success.

TRUST-BASED RELATIONAL INTERVENTION (TBRI)

Developed by Dr. Karyn Purvis and Dr. David Cross, TBRI is a family-based intervention that trains caregivers to provide effective support and treatment for children from hard places. Previous work by van Der

Kolk[4] and Bath[5] determined three main factors that any treatment of complex trauma should address: development of safety, promotion of healing relationships, and teaching of self-management and coping skills. These three factors are foundational to the principles of TBRI: Empowerment—attention to physical needs; Connection—attention to attachment needs; and Correction—attention to behavioral needs. The training teaches these principles to anyone working with children from traumatic places to help caregivers and children learn healthy ways of interacting so that both can play a role in the healing process.[6] While we didn't experience this personally, I've heard great things. It's worth investigating. The Karyn Purvis Institute for Child Development offers trainings and workshops for anyone interested.

HORSEBACK RIDING

Okay, this is a leap from the brain-based therapies above, but I've heard a number of times how much our kids with AD respond to horses! Parents whose kids participate in horseback riding always comment on how well the child does during the sessions. It provides a great break for the family but also has a noticeable effect on the child. Horse therapy has been used for people with PTSD for quite some time, but many are finding that it's a great source of help for their AD kids, too. In the book *Riding Home*, author Tim Hayes talks about the power of horses in affecting the trauma stuck in the brain. He says,

> The emotional healing that begins with the nonjudgmental acceptance of a horse enables patients to feel safe enough to be themselves. This helps bridge the barrier of PTSD isolation and facilitates the social reintegration of talk therapy with another human. A horse can therefore become a crucial and even life-saving component in the beginning stages of PTSD recovery.[7]

This also gives our kids a chance to engage an animal that is under the supervision of a trainer and won't be secretly harmed. Many of our kids show animal cruelty and this provides an opportunity to experience the healing power of animals (without putting one in danger).

. . .

FAITH

One of the common stories I've heard directly from grown children with AD who've found some kind of healing and recovery in their adult lives is their engagement with faith. Specifically, the person of Jesus Christ and the unconditional love demonstrated in the Bible. One young man shared his story with me. Samuel was adopted from an orphanage in Romania. He shared the heartache of the trauma he and his siblings experienced, and how they manifested that in their adoptive home. After years of challenges in the home, his parents realized they weren't enough to meet his needs. He moved to Teen Challenge.

Samuel said,

> The biggest thing that made the change in my life was at a Wednesday night chapel service where the preacher spoke about how no matter what the people threw at Jesus, Jesus still chose to love them and die for their sin. That got me thinking about the way I treated my family and the staff and for the first time in my life, I felt broken and I felt their pain. Honestly, the reality of living a dull and empty life was the leading cause [of change]. I was a very angry and hateful person before I changed and I knew that if I didn't change things in my life one of two things would happen. I would become homeless or become a ward of the state. I had pushed so many people away (including my own family) that it seemed like no one had hope in me anymore. I was living a life of anger attempting to hurt others but in the process only hurt myself. I spent until about 12:00 a.m. crying and praying and seeking God's forgiveness. I spent the next eight months working hard to change my lifestyle and not allow my RAD to control my life. It's been eight years since that day and looking back, it's been one of the hardest eight years in my life! I wanted to make a difference in the lives of troubled boys and worked at several boarding schools over the last six years before starting my own. The other thing that motivated me to change was hope in Christ. I mean, when I actually surrendered myself to Christ and allowed him to bring healing in my life, I felt that

I had a purpose again. What motivated me I hoped might motivate others suffering with RAD and other behavioral issues, and that is why I started a boys home—in hopes of being able to share that hope with others.

Samuel is the founder of Mountain Academy,[8] helping boys between the ages of nine and fourteen discover healing in all areas of life, just as he did. He is a great example of hope. Our kids' stories aren't over! Who knows what, how, or why their stories will pivot, but we keep believing they can.

I recently met Lamont Nash. At three years old, his birth father attempted to kill him. He escaped and was rescued, but from that point on lived a life full of abuse and ongoing trauma. After living in fifteen different homes, Lamont aged out of the system (turned 18 without being adopted) and landed on the streets. After years of searching for his identity in all of the wrong places, Lamont landed in prison. He said that it was an encounter with an unconditionally loving God, who gave His life for him, after all he'd done, that changed him. He founded Playground Training Academy, holding classes and boot-camps for all, intentional about reaching boys from hard places, teaching them discipline, fitness, health, and demonstrating the love of God to all.

These aren't the only stories I've heard of a child's encounter with God being life-changing. But we've also realized it's not enough for the child to be raised in a home of faith. Families of faith have the same behavioral struggles as any other adoptive family. Our kids were raised to know God's unconditional love. But in each story I've heard, it's when the child (or adult) chose to engage the love of Christ that trans-formation occured. And if they struggle to trust us, their human parents, how much more so an invisible God, a father figure, when this is their very fear. Yet, for some, the difference becomes clear and life-changing. We hope that all of our children will engage the truth of God's love, experience it, and see their own lives changed for the best, regardless of their disorders.

. . .

PARENT COACHING

Finally, but certainly not least, we need help. We need therapeutic help. We need support. Community. Healing. Coaching. We need as much encouragement and outlet for our own pain, healing from our own wounds, and new skills and strategies to keep us standing our ground in caring for our kiddos. Not caring from our own broken, beat-up places, but from our healed and healing wounds. We had parent-coaching for a time and it was so helpful. It gave me a chance to cry with someone paid to not judge me. To hear positive feedback and encouragement. Coaching gave me the burst I needed to get through that day, and maybe the next. I could schedule a call anytime and it carried me through a season. We also took advantage of individual and marriage counseling, as well as support groups.

The thing is, at worst, we can't do a single thing to improve our children or their behavior. We can't fix their brains. We can't explain it away. We can't reason with them. We can't hug them long enough to convince them to live loved. At the end of the day, for some of these kids, not a single thing may change.

Except us.

And I totally hate that any of it falls on we, the depleted, empty, exhausted, spent, poured-out parents. We've tried it all and we're tired. And to hear that I am the only one I can change is enough to knock me over the edge. Or so it feels. But the reality is, every time I invested in myself, my own healing, introspection, attachment anxieties, motivations, and chose to step the slightest in a healthier way, things did change. Maybe not with my child's behavior, but with my ability to cope. With my own resiliency. Eventually, I'd built up enough support that even though my kids were at their worst, and that was still painful for me, I could stand on a new foundation. One of learning to trust myself, know my limitations, my contribution to the problem, and dance the dance a little better. To understand love, uphold healthy boundaries, protect my marriage and other family members, and create a space of true love as we sought to help our kids.

Even today, with our kids with AD no longer in the home, the most beneficial work I can do for them is to work on myself. We helped them navigate the new life of adulting. Met with the same challenges in a new form. And anytime I felt triggered, I had a toolbox specifically marked "Marcy." Where I could recognize why I felt triggered, listen to the message I was believing, usually a lie that I was making up about the situation, and move toward a more healthy response. Same kids, but a more whole me.

I know this might sound impossible. Where do you find the time? The money? The resources? But if you do nothing else, do this. Fund this. Choose this. Choose helping *you* and believe me, your outlook will take a turn for the better. And who knows, maybe your kids will catch on and make some changes themselves.

CHAPTER 18

WHEN LOVE IS ENOUGH: REDEFINING LOVE

O ne of the harder lessons that chased us down was around our definition of love. As a person of faith, I believe that love is sacrificial. Jesus says that there is no greater love than laying down your life for your brother or friend (John 15:13). To think of others more highly than of yourself (Philippians 2:4). That if someone slaps your cheek, to give them the other one too (Luke 6:29). He modeled this with His own life and death and life, again. He gave up his very life so that I could live (John 3:16-17).

So certainly this is true with our kids, too, right?

With this sacrificial view of love in mind, twisted together with my need to be liked and approved of, I set out on a heroic journey to prove my love, God's love, to these kids. I missed opportunities to truly love them because of my misconception of it. Or rather, my misconception of my ability to love to the fullest. Our love was certainly sacrificial. We nearly gave up our marriage, our other children, our friendships and relationships, our reputations, our time and energy. But it wasn't necessarily love. It was based on a cultural construct and, to be honest, sometimes on my fears of what other people would think. What would people think if I sent my son to a residential treatment facility? That's not what good parents do, is it? What would people think if they walked into my bathroom and my cupboards were all locked? Would they think I'm crazy? Some of my "love" was really fear.

And as I've studied the work of Dr. Brené Brown and Dr. Cloud and Dr. Townsend, I've come to see that having healthy boundaries is the most compassionate thing we could have done. Knowing our capacity and living from within it *is* love. Exceeding that and living from a place of resentment, anger, frustration, regret, and confusion doesn't serve anyone, and it certainly isn't loving. One of my favorite lines from a video called *Boundaries* with Dr. Brené Brown says,

> The most compassionate people I had interviewed... were also the absolutely most boundaried... I am not as sweet as I used to be, but I'm far more loving.[1]

It's a video I've had to watch on repeat to wrap my brain around this new construct. My saying "yes" because of obligation or people-pleasing or anything other than my sheer desire is going to be unloving. I must know my motivation, and if my motivation isn't love from within a healthy understanding of myself, and an integrity to live honestly, then it's not love.

I see this in the Bible as well. Where I had always focused on the sacrificial aspects of love, I had conveniently glossed over the boundaries in the Bible. And to be honest, I've always kind of hated the word "boundaries." It feels so mean. But the reality is, they are the kindest thing you can offer and uphold. I truly believe this now. And I see this demonstrated in the love of Christ. Yes, He gave the ultimate sacrifice—His very life, because that's what we needed. Yet, in His sacrifice, He didn't compromise on the boundaries. Sin is still sin, the way to heaven is still the way to heaven. His gift to us bridged a gap. Made a way. Reconciled us.

The death of my marriage, my own mental health, or that of my other children will not serve my kids with AD. It won't serve your kids with

AD. The death of these things does not translate to love for your child. In fact, it's the opposite.

Love is seeking the best for the other person. And sometimes what is best for them doesn't feel good for us or them! It might be questioned by people who don't get it. It might feel like quitting. Bowing out. Failing. I'm sure many thought the death of Jesus looked like a big fat failure. That was the opposite of what people at the time thought God's love would look like. And yet, it was and is the perfect example of kindness compelled by love birthed from genuine desire, seeking a way for us.

Love might look like letting your kiddo try a residential treatment facility so your family can rest and your child can work on healing.

It might mean investing some of those finances and time and energy intentionally into your other children.

It might mean parenting your kid with AD in a unique way, a way that promotes healing and bonding, even if it doesn't look typical.

It might mean releasing your child to care that has more capacity, resources, and support.

It might mean taking a second mortgage on your house to pay for treatment.

And it might mean not taking a second mortgage on your house for another treatment.

It depends on what best serves your child *and* your family. And often, when it's our demonstrations of love that are triggering their trauma, they are not going to find healing exclusively in our home. We often need a reset to regroup ourselves and come back to it in a healthier space. And they need a reset to know we mean business.

One of my kids needed help, and we didn't have the resources financially, emotionally, or physically. We got creative and found work that gave our child a few weeks away from home. We were *empty*. Within a week they were ready to fire our kid, and after two weeks, they did.

They tried hard to work with our teen, but our teen wouldn't/couldn't do it. So our teen came home, and I about died. I was so tired. I had nothing left to give. At that very moment, we had an opportunity to send our teen, for $20,000, to a 3-month program for kids just like him.

But no! That would mean I was giving up on love! Betraying a God who was willing to give His very life for mine. The least I could do was show my kid that same love! And what if people thought I was a failure? What if *I* thought I was a failure? Because failures can't find enough love to heal their kid, so they send them away! So instead, we spent $5000 from our savings and hired a family coach through the same program. An outpatient service. As far as the service for our teenager, nothing changed. And in fact, where I'd trusted that this program understood kids with RAD, our family coach was immediately triangulated. So much so that I requested a different coach (even though we had been given the head coach and founder of the program). The personal coach was a great help to me, in giving me a safe place to process and get feedback.

In reality, looking back, we needed a break. We needed to heal. Regroup. Get help. And our child needed some stuff too. Time away. An opportunity to operate outside of us for a bit. Feedback from others who could support us without *being* us. Our child needed a break from all the conversations about the emails and phone calls we had every day. And while we'll never know if that program could have delivered on its promises, we do now believe that love would have looked like getting *our* kid inpatient help. It's not a failure to send your child to a program you've researched and believe will respect your need for recovery and their need for help. It's not selfish; it's kind. Keeping our child in the house and trying to keep pouring love from all our emptiness did nothing to improve our situation or our child's. If anything, it further proved that we were weak and untrustworthy.

I don't know what love looks like for your kid, but I challenge you to sit down and really confront your constructs. What are your beliefs around love? What's your definition? Do you believe it's selfish to uphold healthy boundaries? Why? What would it look like to do what's best for them? What messages do you hear about yourself or your family when you think of loving that way? Journal these things, process them with a trusted friend, whatever. But don't let this be the obstacle to help for your family that it was for us.

CHAPTER 19

STRATEGIES THAT WORKED
FOR US AND OTHERS

W hile most treatments don't work permanently, or in the long-term, there are certainly things we can do to ease the load. One website that had the most impact on our parenting housed an article called, *Parenting Children & Teens with Reactive Attachment Disorder.*[1] We found that we visited the article so often, that we finally printed it and marked it all up. What were we doing already? What were the major shifts we needed to make? What matched our child's particular nuances? The whole website is great for resources, as is The Institute for Attachment site.[2] Make these two sites your Best Online Friends Forever (BOFF).

We all know by now that traditional or typical ways of parenting do not work with our kiddos. So what does work? While that's a bit of a guessing game, aside from working on ourselves, there are a handful of strategies that served our family well. If nothing else, they remove the consequence from being a burden to us and helped them to *serve* us, and hopefully our kids at the same time.

The following include strategies that we personally employed that made our lives a little less crazy. At least in comparison. Some might work for you and your kiddo, some may not. But find the ones that do and love them hard. The techniques we are aiming for should gradually create safety for our kids to have the space to experience the love we have for them. While this will most likely not occur exclusively with these strategies, they create a framework for which a child receiving effective therapeutic support and care can integrate into a home that is actually safe for that child's emotional needs.

Our kids' ideas of safety and belonging are flipped on their head. So in some ways, we can be as safe as humanly possible and they still won't trust us. Forcing their trust is not our responsibility, but creating a safe place should they choose to engage it is.

Here's what we learned didn't work:

Reasoning or logic

Practical information does not change our AD child's mind. In fact, it appears to do the opposite. And it will cost you time and energy, both personally, and from other family members who would love that same time and energy. Additionally, children with AD find our reasoning flipped and illogical and stupid, thus, using it only convinces them that we are unstable and untrustworthy. (HA! Anyone else knocked over by this one? This was my whole strategy!) The brain responds to experience, not information.

Emotionally reacting to their behavior

When kids experience the ability to knock us off kilter, to have a strong effect on our emotions, they are convinced that we can be easily controlled and thus, are not safe. Our frustration and anger demonstrated serve their ideas of grandiosity.

Negotiating

This is only you asking to play a game of manipulation, putting yourself in a position to lose and again prove that you can be controlled and thus are unsafe to trust.

Rescuing the child from the consequences of their behavior

I know, we think we don't do this. I mean, don't we want them to feel it? I remember a time one of our kids wasn't completing homework assignments. We want school success like anyone else, but we'd seen this kid through years of tutors, behavior modification strategies, and hand-holding. She was old enough to take responsibility for assignments and we were done trying to force it to happen. So we stopped. We allowed the consequences of missing school work to fall between our child and the school. She ended up at risk of missing out on extracurricular activities based on low grades. How could I help her out? Should I give her the strategy? Should I hold her hand through the behavior shift? Wouldn't she feel so bad to miss out on band or a sports team? Wouldn't she be so sad? My mama's heart grieved what seemed to be coming. She would not follow through and she'd miss the opportunities. I could step in and make it happen for her *or* let her step up and comply. Our child had every opportunity to do the assignments and didn't. She was ineligible for much-anticipated activities. And she was *still* required to make up the assignments. And we all survived. She learned we meant business. And you know what? The next time a school play came around and she wanted to be involved, her grades improved!

Don't rescue your kids from the consequences. They probably don't feel it as much as you do on their behalves anyway!

Offering unsolicited advice

We so often gave (and give) advice without asking if they wanted it. This becomes another eye-rolling lecture that they tune out. It's us imposing ourselves into their space, taking away the control they so crave. If we can give control in small things, controllable things, we have more impact. Ask your child if they would like your advice before giving it. It forces them to take responsibility for what comes next. It also forces them to take some responsibility for asking for or stating what they want in order to get it. Opportunities to give them responsibility for their actions and decisions are priceless. If they said "no," then we still held them responsible for the information they didn't receive (much like a police officer will still give them a speeding ticket, regardless of whether or not they knew the speed limit). They are responsible for the "yes" as much as the "no." When the tables turn and your child offers you unsolicited advice (orders you around) you can use the same, "I didn't ask for your advice, but when I want it, I'll be sure to ask for it ahead of time."

Don't defend or explain the consequence

We found that we were easily baited into hours-long conversations about why we were justified in handing down a consequence. We all knew why, but our kids were addicted to the adrenaline rush of a challenge and always took these opportunities to try and get us to give them a "high." We learned that all of our explanations were both reasonable (see the first bullet point) and easily used by our kids to chase down rabbit holes. The consequence didn't change, but we were more exhausted for it and had lost precious time with other family members. So we learned to not give explanations but instead to state the information clearly and succinctly. Besides, explanations cause the authority to rest on the reason and not on you as a parent. Hand out the consequence in a business-like matter, not when you're feeling emotionally driven. Take a "time away" for yourself if you need time to find inner calm. Or tag team with your spouse if they're in a better emotional place. Your child can wait in their room until you're ready.

Don't take responsibility for whether or not they receive your love

While it's your job to do the loving, it's *their* job to let it in. I know I was committed to my children knowing they are loved. I didn't realize how much of that is beyond my control! All I can do is offer and extend love. And I can kindly coach my child around receiving it, but the rest is up to them. I *love* a new line that I recently picked up from Lamont Nash (mentioned earlier). "I'm just here to love you." Just be there to love them and tell them so.

HERE'S WHAT WE FOUND DID WORK:

Not caring more about their problems than they do

This was huge for us. I totally care a ton. And they were happy to let me do all the caring while they did all the living. This line gets me every time,

> Nothing is likely to change as long as you are more anxious about your youngster's behavior than she is. So, moms and dads need to be careful not to take on the anxiety that truly belongs to their youngster... In the spirit of counterintuitiveness, acknowledging that your youngster has the freedom and the power to make a mess of her life increases the chances that she won't.[3]

Not giving into pressure to make last-minute decisions

Sometimes our children's manipulation came like a high-pressured sale. They'd make a request that had an immediate need for an answer, usually with only one parent present. This put pressure on one of us to make a quick decision without the other, with the kid pressing for their desire. We finally realized that *their* crisis was not *our* crisis. And we learned that *we* did not have to allow ourselves to be forced into a position of quick decisions. So we asked for 24-hour notice on big decisions. If they didn't give us 24 hours, the answer would just be "no." This forced them to take responsibility for why we would say "no" in a high-pressure situation but also set the expectation that we would think with clear minds about what was being asked of us.

Help with connections

Our kids seem to lack the ability to make connections between just about anything. They don't recognize cause and effect, so the connection between their choices and the outcome doesn't exist. They don't make connections between their feelings and what triggered them, or how that led to a behavior choice, and so on. Everything just seems to happen to them. They choose to lie but can't understand why people don't believe them. They choose to steal, but can't understand why people lock cupboards and doors when they visit. We continually talked through, drew through, mimed connections for our kids to begin seeing the threads that bind it all.

Speaking of drawing and miming, we learned that since our kids don't receive information well from us verbally, using art or body movements was more effective. My husband is a teacher, so this came naturally to him as a form of teaching from the start. Our kids always responded better when he drew images, diagrams, made lists, whatever, to help them make connections.

Because our kids are so disconnected from themselves, they often don't recognize or know how to name their own feelings. We (and their therapists) spent time labeling and helping them connect to their feelings. And I don't just mean emotions. You may have a kid who is hypersensitive to touch, temperature, personal space, even hunger or pain or a kid who doesn't seem aware of any physical sensations of touch or temperature. We can help our kids make these connections with photo cards of people experiencing different feelings and guessing at their causes. We can role-play situations. We can be mindful of the moments when we see our kids experiencing a feeling but not connecting it to their response or their need. *Yes*, this takes a *lot* of work, but step by step they will begin to make some of these connections.

Do you have a yelling problem? Whisper when you want to yell

First, you'll get their attention, and second, you'll feel a lot better about yourself. When you yell, you are easily tuned out as white noise. But when you whisper, they have to lean in to hear you. Their curiosity is to hear what is being said, which is what you want! It also brings down your heart rate, their heart rate, and soon you'll feel your body responding to your choice to whisper instead of raising your voice.

Work on good eye contact

Eye contact can be tricky. It's an emotional and intimate experience in our Western culture, but it can also feel intimidating and threatening, especially in a power differential, such as between an adult and a child. Helping our kids to work on healthy eye contact with us can help increase their ability to connect with us emotionally, and not just as the obstacles to their freedoms. We can guide them with a gentle touch or by asking for it. Definitely appreciate them when they give it, but don't make this a hill to die on. This will only taint the intimacy of having it when it comes. But until it's more consistently given, gently ask for it.

Healthy touch

Many of the kids with AD we parented were strongly touch-avoidant with us, but overly touchy with strangers or acquaintances. This, sadly, leads to over-sexualized and predatory behavior. We tried to create a space for healthy touch. Some of our kids were older when they joined our family, and touch felt awkward for all of us. We tried to find ways to naturally demonstrate physical affection. Stroking someone's hair during a movie, putting an arm around them on a long walk, high-fives at games, and hugs when they needed comfort. The majority of the time, our affection was met with stiff bodies: stiff arms, necks, and shoulders. But every now and then they'd loosen up a bit and receive it. And sometimes, though mostly just with my husband, they'd put an arm around him or want to snuggle on the couch. On a few occasions, they gave us feedback about wanting more physical affection and this was both shocking (because of their stiffness every time we tried) and encouraging (yay, our efforts mattered!).

Helping our kids experience healthy touch at home and understand the connection between touch and the messages we give through it were key to many of our interactions. We had to help our kids understand that their incessant touching of strangers both broke personal boundaries and communicated messages they didn't always mean to communicate. We had a number of interactions with their school around students expressing discomfort and feeling violated by the over-touching of our children with them. They had to hear this from a variety of settings, not just us. It was most effective when peers gave this feedback directly, but when you're feeling violated, that's not easy to do!

Separating now from then

Because of our kids' disconnected thinking, we have to help them separate the present from the past and future. If you remember, a traumatized brain is stuck in the now. They experience life as though the trauma is still happening in this moment. Their brains are extremely vigilant, working to keep them alive in the threat of the dangers they faced then. They need our help to keep them *present* while separating experiences on their personal timelines. When our kids brought up irrelevant (and sometimes totally false) points from the past, we'd bring them back to right now. "What are you going to do to move forward from here?" Or, "Yes, that happened and it was hard. But today we're dealing with this. So what's your next step from this moment?" (We also noticed they use the past and future to deflect from now. Now is painful and scary and any attempt to keep you away from it is strong). In some cases, drawing out a timeline might help your child. We've pulled out a calendar, or even family photos, to show the distance between events (or to bring accuracy to a faulty memory).

Boundaries on material things

It is okay to prohibit the use of items that aren't being used responsibly. This was strangely new to me. Perhaps again because, really, most of our kids end up with access to very little when we practice this. But the reality is, as long as we continue to permit household items to be used inappropriately they will be used inappropriately, and we will suffer from our own boundarylessness. A line that we loved from *Parenting Children & Teens with Reactive Attachment Disorder* goes like this:

> Toys are for playing with, not for ignoring your parents. It seems you're confused about the purpose of the toys. Therefore, it wouldn't be good for you to keep using the things you're confused about.[4]

We used this line a number of times, especially with devices. The item can be returned for use when 1) the child has shown responsibility with other things for a while and 2) can also verbally promise to use the item appropriately. As soon as they don't, we start again. The goal is that they will learn that they have full control over what items they have access to and which ones they don't.

Find reasons to affirm your kids

Okay, on some days, this felt like, "Good job! You're still blinking!" And other days, when I looked hard, I was surprised by how much I could find that I had been missing in my own bout of negativity. Be careful how you use affirmation. Don't use it manipulatively or to claim victory in a power struggle. "Oh, you did it! Yay! I won!" Rather, express gratitude, how they must be proud of themselves as they're learning how capable they are at this, good they are at that, and move on.

When our kids experienced a hard consequence, like missing the theme park field trip, we expressed empathy by recognizing the hardship their actions have caused them. We communicated that we love them, are there for them, and trust that they'll make a better decision next time.

Put a time limit on consequences in their hands

Another thing that worked for us was letting their reformed behavior determine the end of the consequence. We could say, "You're grounded for a week!" And they'd bear through the week unchanged. But if we said, "You're grounded until all of the stolen items are returned to their proper places," then the length of the grounding was entirely up to them. They could be grounded for five minutes or five years, totally depending on them. It also took the responsibility off of us as task masters and allowed us to be protectors of family relationships.

Temper gift-giving

Have you ever noticed that holidays and family trips are painfully hard with these kids? I'm sure there are multiple reasons why, but one might be a sense of guilt. I don't love that word in relation to this, but essentially, when we give them more than they can give in return, they get angry. One of my friend's kids, on a trip to Disneyland, threw a fit and said, "I didn't want to come to Disneyland anyway!" One of our kids dragged herself through Disneyland like we were making her spend the day getting root canals. I had been so excited to show our kids the things they missed as young children, but they seemed completely incapable of receiving it or enjoying it. When I read that so many of our kids with AD melt during the holidays, gift-giving, and special family trips, and read how they can associate this with guilt, I was shocked! It shows the deep shame they carry, even though they didn't cause their trauma. This same friend's daughter would actually say, after being handed a gift, "You're just trying to manipulate and control me with this gift."

So whether or not it's guilt or some other fear, we began to temper our gift-giving and family experiences to an amount that was less overwhelming. Sometimes, if we knew they were just going to make an event miserable, we'd leave them in the care of someone else and get away and enjoy the trip. It felt awful to not include every child, but we also knew by now that we'd all feel awful together as well.

Be unpredictable

I know that's strange after talking about consistency *but* with our children with AD, this is a little different. Too much consistency actually becomes a breeding ground for manipulation and self-protection from loving parents. A predictable household becomes "unsafe" in the minds of our children because they can control and manipulate it. Therefore, throwing in periodic surprises can disrupt their strategic efforts to control the home. We also choose to be vague sometimes, making it harder for them to figure out what's going on so they can work it. This might mean we say, as a consequence, "*something* is going to happen as a consequence to your choice," but not yet saying what the something is. This also buys you time to think about what you'll do strategically and not reactively. Some families also give short notice when leaving for a holiday or a meal with friends to prevent their child from having time to scheme how to thwart it.

Speak rules in positives

Don't give a list of "don'ts and do's" but instead what they need to do. State the directive simply and clearly and with the expectation that they'll do what is being asked of them. "After school, you will pick all the clothes up off of your floor and place them in the hamper. Thank you for remembering to do this." Thanking them in advance solidifies your belief that they really will accomplish this. We also followed the *Parenting Children & Teens with Reactive Attachment* article by making it clear to our kids that they were also responsible for the rules that *haven't* been discussed. If they simply act without asking about the possible rule, they're still responsible for that rule. This takes the air out of "but I didn't know" as an excuse for why it was okay to act on an impulse.

Cross talking

This was something we found effective. When speaking *to* our kids, they often tuned us out. Their eyes would glaze pretty early in the conversation and we knew they'd checked out. However, when my husband and I spoke to *each other* about the things we wanted our child to hear in their presence, they were very quick to pay attention. (They were often trying to eavesdrop on our conversations anyway, so this played into their "strategy" for gaining useful information). We might use that time to guess at what our child was feeling or experiencing. Sometimes we used it to role-play how the situation *could* have gone, had they done it in a healthy way. They were far more attentive to this approach.

Homeschooling

A number of families have found that traditional school provides an abundance of stimulation and opportunity for chaos in our kids. These families have chosen to bring their kids home for education. While this might sound like the opposite of what you want to do (spend more time with this particular kid), for some, the cost-savings are worth it. There are fewer people to triangulate when you restrict their access to the world. Fewer people questioning your parenting, your love, and your home. At the same time, the structure and consistency of rules and boundaries may provide a better space for learning with your child. I'll be honest, we tried this with one of our two AD kiddos and it was a fail. We still had a baby and a toddler at home when we brought this older child's education to my lap. It was through a charter, so we had some support. But the needs of the child were so intense, that it took away from my ability to do anything well: the care of my toddler and baby and meeting his educational needs. So back to school he went. For some of my other children with AD, homeschooling would have been fine. It depends on your needs, your child's needs, and your school's resources and partnership, but it's a possibility.

———

THERE WERE MANY MORE STRATEGIES WE TOOK FROM VARIOUS articles and friends raising kids with AD. Make sure to visit the websites listed under "Resources" for a full list of techniques you might try in your own home.

I've also spoken with other adoptive families with AD kiddos about strategies they've found helpful in the home. Here they are:

- A lot of securing that I'm the parent and I'm going to take care of them/their needs.
- Proactively seeking them out to offer them physical affection, if they want it.
- Natural consequences and boundaries that are consistent and non-negotiable, without an emphasis on punishment.
- A basic routine where big things are expected but small things might change a bit.
- Not reacting to displays of dramatic emotion or poor behavior.
- Not directly addressing poor behavior (like asking "Did you do this?") but still offering consequences.
- Validating their feelings, showing that I'm interested.
- Making big choices for them, but letting them have control over choosing between A or B with smaller choices. Limiting choices so there aren't too many options.
- Not making a big deal about upcoming events or being vague about details, not giving them advanced notice about family activities that will involve bonding time.
- Taking myself out of situations where I have strong emotions until I am calm and composed enough not to let my upset emotions influence theirs.

- Addressing food allergies. Gluten was highly destabilizing for our son. Corn causes both RAD spouse and child to go from just tearful fits to violent fits.
- Consequence-based parenting and a lot of coaching about social skills has really helped my child. My parenting style of setting and sticking to firm boundaries and consequences has likely helped both kids from a very early age, which has likely helped transform their once violent behavior to much more passive-aggressive or tearful moments instead of raging behaviors.
- Overall we did not see a lot of progress until all of us were in individual and group therapies—an excellent intensive outpatient DBT therapy program where we all have learned to grow and have developed skills. Our AD kid still makes quite a lot of chaos in the home but upside is the rest of us are personally prepared for her acting out.

One final note on parenting techniques with children with AD. As a Behavior Analyst, I often talked with families about the Behavior Burst. Anytime we make a change in our part of the dance, it throws the other person off. They've been used to dancing in tune with our steps, however healthy or dysfunctional those steps have been. With our children, we *expect* that the particular behavior we are working on will *increase* before it will decrease. Why? Because it's always worked before. So they must just need to try a little harder (or a lot) to get you back to your previous dance step.

If you've always responded to tantrums and suddenly you're walking away from the tantruming child until they can calm themselves down, you will likely see an increase in the tantrum itself. I mean, it used to work! So maybe if I'm louder or last longer, I'll get my way again. (The "way" might be attention, control, adrenaline addiction, etc). If at any point you give in and return to your old dance, you teach them that they only have to give it a good go and you'll be right back to your part in the dysfunction. Don't do it! Hold your ground and they will eventually see that you mean business. It's their choice to adjust, and yours to establish a healthy boundary and stick with it.

CHAPTER 20

LOOKING AHEAD

There were many days when we feared the future of our kids. Other days, we gave ourselves permission to dream. But mostly, we saw two very different possibilities for their lives. One where we really did rescue them from a destructive path. They realize we love them, experience it, and attach to us. Then they go to college, get married, have healthy children, and we all live happily ever after. The second path we saw was a repeat of the ones many of their birth families took before them. We saw the possibility of our kids leaving our homes as soon as they were 18 (or before if they could), rejoining birth families who would either benefit from all of our hard work in our shared kids or simply join their lifestyles of drugs, alcohol, gang relations, jail, teen pregnancy, and single parenting or losing their children to foster care. It felt either/or but there's definitely a blend of possibilities on that spectrum. Most of the kids we've parented fell into the latter category.

But we've also seen children with AD find healing in random places. I've heard of young adults with AD where, at the birth of their first child, something suddenly clicked and they were able to bond with their child and find healing in their own broken places. Likewise, there are many children with AD who have a child and nothing changes.

They see their own flesh and blood and nothing happens, recreating attachment dysfunction in their child. If at least one of the parenting pair is able to form a bond with the child immediately, the child may maintain healthy development. While attachment disorders don't seem to be genetic, there are plenty of generations of children living with the disorder. I haven't heard of an indicator of which children with AD will be able to bond with their own children or not. It seems to be something magical when it happens.

While children will never outgrow attachment disorders without treatment, they can (and do) trade the diagnosis for a new one. Many children with AD grow into adults with Narcissistic Personality Disorder or Borderline Personality Disorder.

NARCISSISTIC PERSONALITY DISORDER (NPD) IS A MENTAL disorder characterized by entitlement and self-importance. People with NPD often lack empathy for others, have a strong, inflated sense of self-importance (also known as grandiosity), and thrive on admiration from others. You might also notice a preoccupation with being in power and having prestige, deserving of special treatment and notoriety. In fact, folks with NPD can become very upset if you don't treat them with the high esteem they expect. Interestingly enough, research has shown less gray matter in the part of the brain related to regulating emotions, experiencing and demonstrating empathy, compassion, and cognitive functioning (the left anterior Insula).[1] Less gray matter means less of the good stuff helpful for regulating and responding to emotions in self and others.

As with all of our attachment disorders, the only available treatment for NPD has been talk therapy, and lots of it. Like, years and years of it. It takes recognizing their disconnect from the more typical population, taking responsibility for their actions, and learning to behave in a more socially appropriate way. This means learning to tolerate their own failures and criticisms of others, learning how to manage their emotions, creating realistic goals, and working on healthy relationships with others. Often, NPD has other emotional or mental disorders co-occurring so sometimes medication is used to treat those issues or symptoms.

BORDERLINE PERSONALITY DISORDER (BPD) IS A MENTAL disorder characterized by impulsivity, emotional instability, problems within relationships, and problems with their self-image. It's basically grown up DSED, but now affecting adult relationships, job situations, encounters with the law, etc. People living with BPD often feel emotions very intensely for great lengths of time, making it very difficult to recover to a more stable baseline after triggering events. These folks live with deep insecurity and instability. They deeply fear the abandonment of their friends and family. Their personal relationships are stormy, as they alternate between idealizing the person ("You're my best friend ever!") to devaluing them ("You're the worst person I know."). This leads to a push and pull in their relationships that very few people will stick with. They have intense mood swings and a distorted self-image. The majority of individuals with BPD (75%) are women.[2]

Available treatment for BPD is the same as the rest—lots of talk therapy. Medications might be used to treat coexisting disorders, but nothing has been shown to treat the root of BPD. Some therapies have shown levels of success, especially if they focus on skills like managing emotions and relationship improvement, getting legitimate needs met in a healthy way, and recognizing unhealthy relationship patterns and correcting them.

Listen, I know this is still hard news. And it's not the only possibility. We are still learning, researching, talking, and growing in how to best serve these populations of people. If there's a reassurance here, it's again for you to know that you are not alone and when you took on this kid, you took on a load.

It's not because you're a bad parent or the wrong person for this job. The reality is, the very best parent in the world would have the exact challenges you have. And actually, they'd probably be having more! If our love triggers these kids, then perfecting our love would only perfect their tragic response to it. Yes, we have our part. But our part won't change these kids in the short-term (or even in some cases the long term). We are still responsible for it, to own our part and to do it well. To do it informed as you're doing by reading this book.

And if there's anything we've learned on this journey it is that our love *is* enough, just not in the ways we expected or hoped for.

Our love, little by little, created a tether that matters. My kids still call home, still reach out, in the most uncanny but precious ways, because we loved them relentlessly for all our years together. Our definition of love sometimes failed. We certainly failed. But we kept getting up and trying again, all of us. And even if they say or truly believe they didn't experience love in our homes—they actually did. And that love has shaped them, informed them, ruins them for living fully wrecked. I don't know how that will show up in your kid. I don't know what decisions your love will guide them to in the future. I know there will still be many more mistakes to challenge whether your love mattered. But then they'll call. Or send you a message. Or show up for Christmas. And these are the moments you take note of. Pause and soak it in.

And know that as long as your kid is alive, there is hope! The story isn't over. I've heard many stories, like that of Josh Shipp, a former at-risk foster youth who shared his powerful story of going through foster care and the power of one caring adult who didn't give up. For many years, by all external appearances, he was on a path to addiction and early death. And now he's a teen expert helping families like ours.[3]

Or take Beth Thomas, the infamous "Child of Rage" from the early documentary on RAD from late '80s. She speaks of her own healing experience and how and why she now works with families and children with extreme attachment disorder.[4]

We genuinely do not know who or what our kids will become or how our love mattered. We may never know the specifics. But we know that it lays a powerful foundation. I have come to believe it's not wasted. I can trust that it will be used for some good, even if I don't get to see it myself. Perhaps this sounds overly optimistic, especially for a book with currently incurable disorders! The truth is—we don't know. We can judge what we see in front of us right now, but there are plenty of examples of kids or adults who are never what anyone expected.

So on those hard days when you can't tell if your love makes a difference. Or on those days when you see your love triggering their trauma and all feels lost. Remember to love well, love informed, and love deeply.

RECLAIMING HOPE: A FOSTER-ADOPTION FAMILY SUPPORT NETWORK

Readers of *Reclaiming Hope* and *Parenting Children of Trauma* and I have co-created a highly engaged community of like-minded, desperate-for-hope and help families, from around the world, who daily support each other in fulfilling the great task of loving orphans in their distress to the best of our ability (which we acknowledge is a *team* effort!).

This is a safe place for foster and adoptive parents and support systems to reclaim their homes, their hearts, and their dignity by asking thoughtful questions, sharing their own life lessons as an encouragement to others, and committing to taking regular steps toward a healthier home and sharing it here. All topics are related to healing from our traumatic experiences.

We would love to have you join us!

https://www.facebook.com/groups/rhyouaremore

RESOURCES

The resources in this book are provided for informational purposes only and should not be used to replace the specialized training and professional judgment of a health care or mental health care professional.

Focus Forward Magazine are stories of leaders who were once in the juvenile or child-welfare systems. www.focusforward.org/the-magazine

Josh Shipp is a former at-risk foster youth who now offers training and support for caring adults, curriculum for teens, and writes and speaks regularly for youth and their families. https://joshshipp.com

Samuel, a former at-risk adopted child with RAD found hope and healing and shares that with teenage boys at Mountain Academy School for Boys. www.boysranchacademy.com

The Abide App was recommended by my counselor when I was struggling with C-PTSD. It guides you through breathing exercises with a background sound of your choice (I love the ocean). You can also listen to a guided devotional by topic. abide.co

My Playlist of Music "Fearless and Anxiety Free" bit.ly/2fearless

Feel free to follow my Pinterest board of articles, videos, and resources for raising children with attachment disorder. bit.ly/PinAttach

The Institute for Attachment and Child Development is one of my favorite websites for knowing I'm not alone and getting actual help. www.instituteforattachment.org

The Attachment Trauma Network provides support, education, and advocacy for children of trauma and their families. www.attachment-traumanetwork.org/

City Without Orphans is a local-to-me organization, but they offer great online resources along with local trainings. www.citywithoutor-phans.com

The Massachusetts Adoption Resource Exchange (MARE) has a blog with resources for foster and adoptive families. https://marefamily.blog

The Chaos and the Clutter with Sharla, an adoption advocate, is a blog with some great resources all around. She also has a post on treatment options they've tried. www.thechaosandtheclutter.com

Foster the Family with Jamie is a great wealth of resources for foster-adoptive families. She has a blog, a podcast, a store, and a non profit to "support and encourage foster and adoptive families, mobilize and equip the community and church for foster care and adoption, and advocate for vulnerable children." www.fosterthefamilyblog.com

ATTACh offers great resources for families through annual conferences, online and live trainings, support groups, and a Clinician referral list. www.attach.org

The Sparrow Fund cares for caregivers. They do this though financial assistance as well as additional support like marital assessment to create opportunities for couples to experience healthy dialogue about expectations and growth areas as they prepare to adopt, 1:1 help to locate and line up resources a family may need, coaching with regards to preparing siblings and extended family, and personalized suggestions for building attachment with their new child. Furthermore, The Sparrow Fund hosts a marriage retreat—Together Called—every Spring for foster and adoptive husbands and wives that draws couples from all over the country. For years, The Sparrow Fund has provided care for caregivers of waiting children in orphanages in China as well. While current policies in China make that a challenge, they continue to pursue relationships and opportunities to serve orphanage staff who are serving day in and day out. sparrow-fund.org

Karyn Purvis Institute of Child Development offers resources, trainings, workshops, and lots of information about TBRI. bit.ly/2Uuoina

Playground Training Academy, founded by Lamont Nash in Fresno, California, offers boot camps, obstacle courses & parkour classes, and personal training to help you reach your fitness goals. He uses this gym to mentor boys from hard places. playgroundtrainingacademyllc.com

---

My other books for foster care and adoption support:

Reclaiming Hope: Overcoming the Challenges of Parenting Foster and Adopted Children

Speranza's Sweater: A Child's Journey Through Foster Care and Adoption (a picture book for children)

El suéter de Speranza (spanish edition)

The following lists of "Notes" and "Additional References" are the articles, journals, videos, and posts that I read and reviewed for this book. Make sure to read through and enjoy any articles that support your own additional research. There are some good resources in there!

Please note that footnotes (and resources) in this book contain hyperlinks to external websites as part of bibliographic citations. These hyperlinks have not been activated by the publisher, who cannot verify the accuracy of these links beyond the date of publication.

NOTES

1. ARE YOU GOOD ENOUGH?

1. M&M'S is a trademark of Mars, Incorporated.

2. UNDERSTANDING TRAUMA

1. Weber, K., & Moges, B. (2014, May 7). Parental Influence on the Emotional Development of Children. Retrieved February 16, 2019, from https://my.vanderbilt.edu/developmentalpsychologyblog/2014/05/parental-influence-on-the-emotional-development-of-children/

3. REACTIVE ATTACHMENT DISORDER

1. DeAngelis, T. (2007, March). A new diagnosis for childhood trauma? Retrieved February 16, 2019, from https://www.apa.org/monitor/mar07/diagnosis.aspx
2. Chicot, R., & Winston, R. (2016, February 24). The importance of early bonding on the long-term mental health and resilience of children. Retrieved February 16, 2019, from https://www.ncbi.nlm.nih.gov/pmc/articles/PMC5330336/
3. Reactive Attachment Disorder. (Feb 19, 2019). Traumadissociation.com. Retrieved Feb 19, 2019 from http://traumadissociation.com/rad. Read more: http://traumadissociation.com/rad (License: CC BY-SA 4.0).
4. Brhel, R. (2017, December 01). What Does Attachment Parenting Look Like with an Adopted Child? Retrieved from http://www.mothering.com/articles/ask-the-expert-what-does-attachment-parenting-look-like-with-an-adopted-child
5. Brhel, R. (2017, December 01). What Does Attachment Parenting Look Like with an Adopted Child? Retrieved from http://www.mothering.com/articles/ask-the-expert-what-does-attachment-parenting-look-like-with-an-adopted-child
6. Bayless, K. (n.d.). Reactive Attachment Disorder and Adoption. Retrieved February 16, 2019, from https://www.parents.com/parenting/adoption/reactive-attachment-disorder-and-adoption/

4. DISINHIBITED SOCIAL ENGAGEMENT DISORDER

1. Disinhibited Social Engagement Disorder. (Feb 19, 2019). Traumadissociation.com. Retrieved Feb 19, 2019 from http://traumadissociation.com/disinhibited.html. Read more: http://traumadissociation.com/disinhibited.html (License: CC BY-SA 4.0).

2. Bayless, K. (n.d.). Reactive Attachment Disorder and Adoption. Retrieved February 16, 2019, from https://www.parents.com/parenting/adoption/reactive-attachment-disorder-and-adoption/

5. POST TRAUMATIC STRESS DISORDER

1. Posttraumatic stress disorder. (Feb 19, 2019). Traumadissociation.com. Retrieved Feb 19, 2019 from http://traumadissociation.com/ptsd.html. Read more: http://trau madissociation.com/ptsd.html (License: CC BY-SA 4.0).

6. ACUTE STRESS DISORDER

1. Bryant, R. A. (2011). Acute stress disorder as a predictor of posttraumatic stress disorder: A systematic review. The Journal of Clinical Psychiatry, 72, 233-239.
2. Sexual Abuse: An Epidemic in Foster Care Settings? (n.d.). Retrieved February 17, 2019, from https://www.hg.org/legal-articles/sexual-abuse-an-epidemic-in-foster-care-settings-6703
3. Acute Stress Disorder. (Feb 19, 2019). Traumadissociation.com. Retrieved Feb 19, 2019 from http://traumadissociation.com/acutestressdisorder.html. Read more: http://traumadissociation.com/acutestressdisorder.html (License: CC BY-SA 4.0).
4. Litz, B., Hundert, C., & Jordan, A. (n.d.). Acute Stress Disorder. Retrieved February 17, 2019, from http://www.dartmouth.edu/-ajordan/papers/Litz, Hundert, & Jordan - ASD entry.pdf
5. Bressert, S. (2018, September 08). Acute Stress Disorder Symptoms. Retrieved February 17, 2019, from https://psychcentral.com/disorders/acute-stress-disorder-symptoms/

7. ADJUSTMENT DISORDERS

1. Adjustment Disorders. (Feb 19, 2019). Traumadissociation.com. Retrieved Feb 19, 2019 from http://traumadissociation.com/adjustment.html (License: CC BY-SA 4.0).

9. SURVIVAL SKILLS

1. Pathological liars found to have less gray matter. (2011, October 19). Retrieved February 17, 2019, from https://www.news-medical.net/news/2005/10/18/13840.aspx
2. Noonan, N. (2015, February 24). How an adoptive mom becomes a ""nurturing enemy"" (the unfortunate effects of reactive attachment disorder). Retrieved February 17, 2019, from https://www.instituteforattachment.org/how-an-adoptive-mom-becomes-a-nurturing-enemy-the-unfortunate-effects-of-reactive-attachment-disorder/
3. Noonan, N. (2015, February 24). How an adoptive mom becomes a ""nurturing enemy"" (the unfortunate effects of reactive attachment disorder). Retrieved

February 17, 2019, from https://www.instituteforattachment.org/how-an-adoptive-mom-becomes-a-nurturing-enemy-the-unfortunate-effects-of-reactive-attachment-disorder/

11. IMPACT ON OUR KIDS WITH ATTACHMENT DISORDER

1. Cloud, H., & Townsend, J. (2017). *Boundaries* (p. 305). Grand Rapids, MI: Zondervan.

12. IMPACT ON US: PHYSICAL

1. Frank, P. (2016, June 16). Study Says Making Art Reduces Stress, Even If You Kind Of Suck At It. Retrieved February 17, 2019, from https://www.huffingtonpost.com/entry/study-says-making-art-reduces-stress_us_576183ece4b09c926cfdccac
2. Chang, L. (2018, December 12). Cortisol: What It Does & How To Regulate Cortisol Levels. Retrieved February 17, 2019, from https://www.webmd.com/a-to-z-guides/what-is-cortisol
3. How Technology Impacts Sleep Quality. (n.d.). Retrieved February 17, 2019, from https://www.sleep.org/articles/ways-technology-affects-sleep/
4. Feldman, S. (n.d.). Alleviating Anxiety, Stress and Depression with the Pet Effect. Retrieved February 17, 2019, from https://adaa.org/learn-from-us/from-the-experts/blog-posts/consumer/alleviating-anxiety-stress-and-depression-pet
5. Borchard, T. J. (2018, July 08). Spirituality and Prayer Relieve Stress. Retrieved February 17, 2019, from https://psychcentral.com/blog/spirituality-and-prayer-relieve-stress/

13. IMPACT ON US: MENTAL

1. http://www.proqol.org/uploads/ProQOL_5_English_Self-Score_3-2012.pdf

14. IMPACT ON US: EMOTIONAL

1. www.ministrysafe.com
2. Why Utah now has first 'free-range' parenting law. (2018, May 06). Retrieved February 17, 2019, from https://www.bbc.com/news/world-us-canada-43997862
3. Noonan, N. (2015, February 24). How an adoptive mom becomes a ""nurturing enemy"" (the unfortunate effects of reactive attachment disorder). Retrieved February 17, 2019, from https://www.instituteforattachment.org/how-an-adoptive-mom-becomes-a-nurturing-enemy-the-unfortunate-effects-of-reactive-attachment-disorder/

16. IMPACT ON BIRTH CHILDREN

1. Williams, E. (2018, June 29). The Impact of Fostering and Adoption on Birth Children - Part 1 (QPI Training Video). Retrieved February 17, 2019, from http://center-video.forest.usf.edu/video/qpi/florida/theimpact/start.html
2. Williams, E. (2018, June 29). The Impact of Fostering and Adoption on Birth Children - Part 1 (QPI Training Video). Retrieved February 17, 2019, from http://center-video.forest.usf.edu/video/qpi/florida/theimpact/start.html

17. CURRENT TREATMENT OPTIONS

1. Schwartz, A. (2017, November 17). Healing Attachment Trauma with EMDR Therapy. Retrieved February 17, 2019, from https://maibergerinstitute.com/healing-attachment-trauma-with-emdr-therapy/
2. Brain Spotting. (2018, March 8). Retrieved February 17, 2019, from https://www.goodtherapy.org/learn-about-therapy/types/brainspotting-therapy
3. Brain Training-EEG Biofeedback. (n.d.). Retrieved February 17, 2019, from http://www.obsidianhealwell.com/neurofeedback.html
4. Kinniburgh K., Blaustein M., Spinazzola J., van der Kolk B. Attachment, self-regulation, and competency: A comprehensive framework for intervention with childhood complex trauma. Psychiatric Annals. 2005;35(5):424–430.
5. Bath H. The three pillars of trauma-informed care. Reclaiming Children and Youth. 2008;17(3):17–12.
6. Purvis, K. B., Cross, D. R., Dansereau, D. F., & Parris, S. R. (2013, October). Trust-Based Relational Intervention (TBRI): A Systemic Approach to Complex Developmental Trauma. Retrieved April 5, 2019, from https://www.ncbi.nlm.nih.gov/pmc/articles/PMC3877861/#R67
7. Hayes, T. (n.d.). Trauma Healing - Riding Home, The Power of Horses to Heal. Retrieved February 17, 2019, from https://www.ridinghome.com/trauma-healing/
8. https://www.boysranchacademy.com/

18. WHEN LOVE IS ENOUGH: REDEFINING LOVE

1. Andersom, Z., & Brown, B. (2017, March 16). Brene Brown. Retrieved February 17, 2019, from https://www.youtube.com/watch?v=BESvQB6J5rc

19. STRATEGIES THAT WORKED FOR US AND OTHERS

1. Hutten, M. (n.d.). Parenting Children & Teens with Reactive Attachment Disorder. Retrieved February 17, 2019, from http://www.reactiveattachment-disorder.com/2009/07/parenting-children-with-reactive.html
2. https://www.instituteforattachment.org/

3. Hutten, M. (n.d.). Parenting Children & Teens with Reactive Attachment Disorder. Retrieved February 17, 2019, from http://www.reactiveattachment-disorder.com/2009/07/parenting-children-with-reactive.html

4. Hutten, M. (n.d.). Parenting Children & Teens with Reactive Attachment Disorder. Retrieved February 17, 2019, from http://www.reactiveattachment-disorder.com/2009/07/parenting-children-with-reactive.html

20. LOOKING AHEAD

1. Gregory, C. (2019, February 5). What to Do About Narcissistic Personality Disorder? Retrieved February 17, 2019, from https://www.psycom.net/personality-disorders/narcissistic/

2. Borderline Personality Disorder. (2017, December). Retrieved February 17, 2019, from https://www.nami.org/learn-more/mental-health-conditions/borderline-personality-disorder

3. Shipp, J. (2017, October 30). The Power of One Caring Adult. Retrieved February 17, 2019, from https://joshshipp.com/one-caring-adult/

4. Kim, M., & Thomas, B. (2015, April 28). The People Speak. Retrieved February 17, 2019, from https://bbsradio.com/podcast/people-speak-april-28-2015

ADDITIONAL REFERENCES

Adjustment disorders. (2017, October 25). Retrieved February 19, 2019, from https://www.mayoclinic.org/diseases-conditions/adjustment-disorders/symptoms-causes/syc-20355224

Applied Behavioral Analysis. (n.d.). Five Coping Strategies for RAD Parents. Retrieved February 20, 2019, from https://www.appliedbehavioranalysisprograms.com/lists/five-coping-strategies-parents-kids-rad-reactive-attachment-disorder/

Bergland, C. (2013, January 22). Cortisol: Why the "Stress Hormone" Is Public Enemy No. 1. Retrieved February 20, 2019, from https://www.psychologytoday.com/us/blog/the-athletes-way/201301/cortisol-why-the-stress-hormone-is-public-enemy-no-1

Bhandari, S. (2018, May 20). Mental Health: Reactive Attachment Disorder. Retrieved February 19, 2019, from https://www.webmd.com/mental-health/mental-health-reactive-attachment-disorder

Bourg Carter, S. (2014, July 28). Are You Suffering from Compassion Fatigue? Retrieved February 20, 2019, from https://www.psychologytoday.com/us/blog/high-octane-women/201407/are-you-suffering-compas-sion-fatigue

Children's Hospital. (2014, August 24). Adjustment Disorders. Retrieved February 19, 2019, from https://www.chop.edu/conditions-diseases/adjustment-disorders

Drake, M., Jr. (n.d.). Specific Trauma and Stressor-Related Disorders DSM-5 309.8 (F43). Retrieved February 19, 2019, from https://www.theravive.com/therapedia/specific-trauma-and-stressor-related-disorders-dsm--5-309.8-(f43)

Gattuso, R. (2018, March 28). Complex PTSD: How a New Diagnosis Differs From Standard PTSD. Retrieved February 19, 2019, from https://www.talkspace.com/blog/complex-ptsd-versus-standard-ptsd/

Hambrick, B. (2015, August 31). 12 Factors that Contribute the Intensity of Trauma's Impact. Retrieved February 19, 2019, from http://bradhambrick.com/12-factors-that-contribute-the-intensity-of-traumas-impact/

Hopper, J. (2018, April 03). Freezing During Sexual Assault and Harassment. Retrieved February 27, 2019, from https://www.psycholo-gytoday.com/us/blog/sexual-assault-and-the-brain/201804/freezing-during-sexual-assault-and-harassment

Hutten, M. (n.d.). Parenting Children & Teens with Reactive Attachment Disorder. Retrieved February 19, 2019, from http://www.reactiveattachment-disorder.com/2012/03/control-and-limit-setting-for-rad.html

Jonkman, C., Oosterman, M., Schuengel, C., Bolle, E., Boer, F., & Lindauer, R. (2014, July 15). Disturbances in attachment: Inhibited and disinhibited symptoms in foster children. Retrieved February 19, 2019, from https://capmh.biomedcentral.com/articles/10.1186/1753-2000-8-21

Kivi, R., & Legg, T. (2017, November 28). Acute Stress Disorder. Retrieved February 19, 2019, from https://www.healthline.-com/health/acute-stress-disorder#prevention

Kostelyk, S. (2018, February 05). What I Wish You Knew About Parenting a Child With RAD. Retrieved February 20, 2019, from https://www.thechaosandtheclutter.com/archives/wish-knew-parenting-child-rad

Kraybill, O. (2018, August 15). What Is Developmental Trauma? Retrieved February 20, 2019, from https://www.psychologytoday.-com/us/blog/expressive-trauma-integration/201808/what-is-develop-mental-trauma

Leonard, J. (2018, August 28). Complex PTSD: Symptoms, behaviors, and recovery. Retrieved February 19, 2019, from https://www.medical-newstoday.com/articles/322886.php

Mayo Clinic. (2018, June 28). Borderline Personality Disorder. Retrieved February 20, 2019, from https://www.mayoclinic.org/dis-eases-conditions/borderline-personality-disorder/symptoms-causes/syc-20370237

Mirza, K., Mwimba, G., Pritchett, R., & Davidson, C. (2016, June 6). Association between Reactive Attachment Disorder/Disinhibited Social Engagement Disorder and Emerging Personality Disorder: A Feasibility Study. Retrieved February 19, 2019, from https://www.ncbi.nlm.nih.gov/pmc/articles/PMC4913055/

Morin, A., & Gans, S. (2018, September 17). Kids Who Are Too Friendly With Strangers May Have This Disorder. Retrieved February 19, 2019, from https://www.verywellmind.com/what-is-disinhibited-social-engagement-disorder-4138254

Noonan, N. (2017, February 01). 4 societal problems that leave kids with reactive attachment disorder stuck in "Groundhog Day".

Retrieved February 19, 2019, from https://www.instituteforattachment.org/4-societal-problems-that-leave-kids-with-reactive-attachment-disorder-stuck-in-groundhog-day/

Pasadena Villa. (2018, April 30). Mental Health vs. Emotional Health...Are They Related? Retrieved from https://www.pasadenavilla.com/2018/02/26/mental-health-vs-emotional-healthare-they-related/

Purvis, K. (2017, June 15). TBRI®: Trust-Based Relational Intervention®. Retrieved April 5, 2019, from https://www.youtube.com/watch?v=FWScSJKjn1A

Purvis, K. B., Cross, D. R., Dansereau, D. F., & Parris, S. R. (2013, October). Trust-Based Relational Intervention (TBRI): A Systemic Approach to Complex Developmental Trauma. Retrieved April 5, 2019, from https://www.ncbi.nlm.nih.gov/pmc/articles/PMC3877861/

Reactive Attachment Disorder. (Feb 19, 2019). Traumadissociation.com. Retrieved Feb 19, 2019 from http://traumadissociation.com/rad

ReGain. (2018, September 4). What Is Attachment Therapy, And How Does It Work? Retrieved February 20, 2019, from https://www.regain.us/advice/attachment/what-is-attachment-therapy-and-how-does-it-work/

Schwartz, A. (2017, December 20). The Neurobiology of Trauma. Retrieved February 19, 2019, from https://drarielleschwartz.com/the-neurobiology-of-trauma-dr-arielle-schwartz/#.XGz4tJNKjOR

Seltzer, L. (2015, July 08). Trauma and the Freeze Response: Good, Bad, or Both? Retrieved February 27, 2019, from https://www.psychologytoday.com/us/blog/evolution-the-self/201507/trauma-and-the-freeze-response-good-bad-or-both

Sollitto, L. (2018, November 05). The one thing most people don't know about adoption. Retrieved February 19, 2019, from https://www.instituteforattachment.org/the-one-thing-most-people-dont-know-about-adoption/

Stinson, F. S., Dawson, D. A., Goldstein, R. B., Chou, S. P., Huang, B., Smith, S. M., . . . Grant, B. F. (2008, July). Prevalence, correlates, disability, and comorbidity of DSM-IV narcissistic personality disorder: Results from the wave 2 national epidemiologic survey on alcohol and related conditions. Retrieved February 20, 2019, from https://www.ncbi.nlm.nih.gov/pubmed/18557663

Thorpe, M. (2017, April 17). 11 Natural Ways to Lower Your Cortisol Levels. Retrieved February 20, 2019, from https://www.healthline.com/nutrition/ways-to-lower-cortisol#section8

Williams, K. (2018, July 18). When your bucket overflows as you raise a child with reactive attachment disorder (and how to help parents you know). Retrieved February 19, 2019, from https://www.instituteforattachment.org/when-your-bucket-overflows/

Zeanah, Charles & D Mary, M & Gleason, Mary Margaret. (2010). Reactive Attachment Disorder: a review for DSM-V. https://www.researchgate.net/publication/228683818_Reactive_Attachment_Disorder_a_review_for_DSM-V

Zeanah, C. H., & Gleason, M. M. (2015, March). Annual research review: Attachment disorders in early childhood—clinical presentation, causes, correlates, and treatment. Retrieved February 19, 2019, from https://www.ncbi.nlm.nih.gov/pubmed/25359236

ABOUT THE AUTHOR

Marcy Pusey is an award-winning author of several bestselling books for adults and children, an international two-time TEDx speaker, and the Founder of Miramare Ponte Press. With her passion for story-telling and her commitment to uplifting others, Marcy loves to inspire her readers with powerful tales that touch the heart and stir the soul. She also enjoys helping fellow authors pursue their writing dreams by providing them with coaching, consultation, and publishing services.

Marcy has spent her whole life helping others. Through her work as a Certified Rehabilitation Counselor and Certified Trauma and Resilience Practitioner, she helps people discover the emotional tools and support they need to grow beyond trauma and embrace their lives to the fullest. Her two TEDx talks, "How Story Empowers Kids to Shape our World" & "You Are More Than Your Traumatic Experiences", have garnered international attention.

Over the last twenty years, Marcy has worked with children, adults, families, and couples through private practices, group homes, foster family agencies, community-based services, wrap-around programs, workshops, trainings, and speaking. In addition, Marcy fostered multiple children, in addition to adopting two and birthing two.

Marcy is proud to lead a life of adventure. She's tossed pizzas for a pizzeria, sang in a musical, advocated for families with special needs, made appearances in a few movies, and mimed with balloon animals at the Halifax Busker Festival. For more information about Marcy and her work, visit her website at www.marcypusey.com or www.miramare-pontepress.com

ALSO BY MARCY PUSEY

For Adults:

Reclaiming Hope: Overcoming the Challenges of Parenting Foster and Adopted Children

The Abundance of Less: A Social Experiment in Not Buying Anything New for One Year

While We Slept: Finding Hope and Healing After Homicide

Overcoming Writer's Block: The Writer's Guide to Beating the Blank Page

---

Children's Books:

Tercules

Weirdo and Willy

According to Corban (also in German)

Bath Time Magic (Book 2 of the *According to Corban* series)

Speranza's Sweater: A Child's Journey Through Foster Care and Adoption (children's picture book) (also in Spanish)

Forever Homes

URGENT PLEA!

Thank you for purchasing my book!

I really appreciate all of your feedback, and love hearing what you have to say.

I need your input to make the next version better.

Please leave a helpful review on Amazon and Goodreads.

Thanks so much!!

Made in the USA
Las Vegas, NV
22 September 2023

77948345R00121